NUCLEAR WEAPONS

and the
CONFLICT of CONSCIENCE

NUCLEAR
WEAPONS

CHARLES SCRIBNER'S SONS, NEW YORK

and

THE
CONFLICT
of
CONSCIENCE

EDITED BY JOHN C. BENNETT

Contents

Contents

Foreword

Tʜɪs volume was projected because there has been a noticeable silence in this country about the ethical issues involved in the nuclear arms race and in the possibility of nuclear war. There is national anxiety about the threat of nuclear catastrophe but even this is often hidden or suppressed. Robert W. Tucker in his book, *The Just War,* suggests that the response by Americans to the prospect of employing force even under the conditions of the nuclear age has "all too frequently reflected the complacent belief that the moral dilemmas attending the employment of force may be clearly resolved and that political success may be easily equated with moral achievement" (p. 104).

It is difficult for the American people to believe in their hearts that they may ever be the victims of an overwhelming disaster; until now they have been spared as they have watched other peoples touch the depths of suffering. It is even more difficult for most of us to realise that, if once our nation decided to use force, the justice of the cause would not cancel the moral horror in the use of nuclear weapons. The wars that have been fought in this century have been regarded as moral crusades and most Americans have been easily convinced that the use of any weapons against any targets was justified if it would insure victory for the cause. When in the Korean war our government held back on both weapons and targets and decided not to push on to victory there was much frustration in the land.

Apart from pacifists whose concern about the ethical issue raised by nuclear weapons can be taken for granted there are two circles in this country where there has been public discussion of the conflict of conscience over nuclear weapons. Many nuclear scientists, because of their full awareness of the consequences of nuclear war and of atmospheric nuclear tests, have been much torn in their minds and consciences as they have had to face the moral meaning of their involvement in extensions of the government's nuclear program. This inner conflict felt by the scientists was especially acute when the decision was made to develop the hydrogen bomb. In recent years, though there has been much objection in the scientific community to nuclear tests, especially to atmospheric tests, the expressions

7

of moral agony by distinguished scientists have been muted. Their earlier protests were overwhelmed by events. The chapter by Dr. Inglis shows, however, the vivid awareness of the effects of the use of nuclear weapons which the nuclear scientists continue to keep before policy-makers and the public.

A second circle in which we can find some articulate conflict of conscience is a limited group of Roman Catholic theologians and moralists. The Roman Catholic Church has been the chief guardian of the theory of the "just war" which involves moral limits in regard to the methods used in warfare. The tradition of the "just war" belongs to Christendom as a whole. Its chief author was St. Augustine who is owned as "Church Father" by both Catholics and Protestants. Yet, the most precise thinking about the casuistry of the conduct of war has been done by Catholics.

Since World War II, Roman Catholics have been involved in an intensive discussion of this issue. The best presentation of this discussion in the United States is the volume, *Morality and Modern Warfare* (edited by William J. Nagle, Helicon Press, 1960). It is significant that the one member of the Atomic Energy Commission who spoke most forcefully on the moral aspects of nuclear war was the late Thomas E. Murray who, as a Catholic layman, reflected this discussion within his Church. Roman Catholic thinkers are also influenced by their tendency to see Communism as an absolute ideological enemy that cannot be expected to be changed by history. While Catholics are not agreed on this, it is certainly the dominant view of Communism among American Catholics and makes it especially difficult for them to be guided by their own conception of moral limits in warfare if the enemy is expected to be a Communist nation. Since they do not renounce these limits in principle, the problem of conscience is acute for many sensitive and sophisticated Catholic thinkers. I think that the neglect of the tradition of the just war by Protestants has prevented them from being as articulate on this issue as Catholic thinkers. They have usually found the appearance of precision in Catholic moral thinking on these issues of doubtful relevance to real decisions. Indeed, in recent years I have noted a puzzled silence among Protestants who are not committed pacifists. Protestants who are non-pacifists, unless they develop some basis for moral limits in warfare, are likely to be carried along by events and to find themselves giving reluctant assent to everything that the government regards as necessary from the point of view of military strategy. Indeed, except for a few protests that were soon forgotten, neither Catholics nor Protestants did much better during the Second World War up to the time of Hiroshima. The use of the atomic bombs on Japan did cause many Protestants and Catholics to protest after the event.

There is a difference of moral climate in the United States from many other countries in regard to nuclear weapons. For example, there is much more radical discussion of the issue in Britain and West Germany and various other countries. Even among Catholics there is a difference. The symposium by British Catholics entitled *Morals and Missiles: Catholic Essays on the Problem of War Today* (James Clarke, London, 1959) is dominated by nuclear pacifism. I think that one major difference between sensitive and thoughtful Americans and their counterparts in some other countries arises from the fact that the United States is the only nation that has the power that can offset the power of the Soviet Union. It is much easier to raise the most radical questions about nuclear armaments and nuclear war if one's country does not have the power or the responsibility to prevent a monopoly of this decisive form of military power in the Communist world. I believe that these radical questions ought to be raised, but I also understand those whose chief fear is that, if they are raised, there will be some weakening of the deterrent to Russian or Chinese pressures.

In the nineteen fifties it was easy to overlook the moral problem of nuclear war because there was confidence that the possession of the weapons would prevent war. This was part of the rationale of the report of the Commission on Weapons of Mass Destruction which met under the Chairmanship of Bishop Angus Dun. This report, of which I was one of the signers, was a landmark in Protestant thinking about nuclear weapons but it was dominated by the conviction that nuclear war could most surely be prevented by the strength of the American nuclear deterrent. This kept its authors from facing the full depth of the nuclear dilemma as it will be seen in this decade.

Similarly, the many secular books that deal with nuclear weapons and national security are mostly written on the assumption that if we keep up the strength of our nuclear deterrent, war can be prevented. Many of them seek a shift in our military policy from emphasis upon all-out nuclear war to emphasis upon limited war. It is assumed that this is the surest way in which to prevent the war that is most feared, provided that all is done against the background of the ultimate deterrent. In the nineteen sixties it may well be that these hopeful assumptions will be less convincing than in the previous decade. The danger that all-out nuclear war may come from a misunderstanding by either side of the other's intention or from escalation in the case of a limited military operation is now emphasized. The confidence that a war in which tactical nuclear weapons are used can be kept limited seems to be waning. In much of this discussion of strategy the most hard-boiled "realists" have often assumed an optimism about human rationality under stress that is not much more credible than the optimism about human morality among the "idealists." I have no doubt that within this decade, if the nuclear arms race continues uncontrolled and new families of weapons induce new degrees of fear, this optimism of the "realists" will tend to disappear and we will be forced to face the nuclear dilemma in its starkness.

There is frequent use of the idea of acceptable damage in current discussions of nuclear weapons and it seems to have as its meaning the amount of damage that can be absorbed by a nation, including our own, and still permit its survival as recognizably the same nation. But there is a neglect in these discussions of the quality of life in the nation that is likely to survive. There must finally be some moral meaning to the word "acceptable." It cannot always be used as a quantitative abstraction. The question must be raised: what damage is it morally acceptable to permit our own people to suffer or to inflict on the people of another nation? But this question is seldom asked especially as it affects the adversary. One reason that it may not be asked is that, even to ask it, might seem to weaken the effect of the deterrent. Also it may be felt rather than said that, if the worst does come, we and the people of the enemy nation will be engulfed in a common tragedy to which nothing that is said in advance will have much relevance, and the choices that will be made within the catastrophic situation will be controlled by a kind of tragic necessity that will transcend moral distinctions. This feeling may be natural and yet, when it is made articulate, I doubt if as responsible beings we can live with it for long.

There is another reason for pushing aside the ethical question or suppressing the conflict of conscience involved in the nuclear dilemma. Our adversaries seem implacable. They are not believed to have any conflict of conscience. The only language that they are expected to understand is the language of the strongest deterrent needed to cause them to realize that any aggression on their part will result in "unacceptable damage" to them. There is validity in this attitude on our part, and yet we cannot live with it indefinitely. There is a nuclear dilemma. One side of this dilemma is the implacability of the adversary and the threat that at least by blackmail his power may be extended unless he finds himself limited by an unyielding force. But the other side of this dilemma can only be spelled out in terms of the human consequences of nuclear war, even of the nuclear arms race itself, and this cannot be done without raising the question of the degree of destruction a nuclear war might cause us to inflict on human beings in another nation. If there is no discussion of these matters, policy is likely to become partly blind and to put too much emphasis on one side of the dilemma. Also, in the course of decades there is danger that there would be a serious atrophy of conscience.

This book does not offer any one set of answers to these questions. We hope that it will stimulate discussion because of the differences which it represents. The authors share a common concern that these questions be raised.

The first two chapters by John Herz and David Inglis are intended to state the problem in the light of the history of warfare, the current international situation and scientific estimates about the effect of nuclear weapons. Then there are four chapters which are intended to deal with assumptions which should govern the attempt to find solutions to our problem. Not one of them defines a full political policy. Those by Kenneth Thompson, Erich Fromm and myself are arranged in their present order because they seem to represent a spectrum of points of view. Probably most readers will find their own point of view somewhere within the range suggested by these three chapters. Paul Ramsey's chapter and mine are similar in their outcome but he was asked to deal specifically with the tradition of the "just war" and to see how far it may have applicability to our situation. The final chapter by Roger Shinn dicusses the effect of man's new destructive powers on the meaning of history and on faith in providence and human destiny.

There is no chapter in this volume by an absolute pacifist. Those who represent this tradition have thought about the ethical aspect of the nuclear dilemma with persistence and acuteness. The pressure of their consciences upon those who are not absolute pacifists helps to keep the latter from the convenient forgetting of many issues. However, it is not news that those who have always been pacifists now oppose both the possession and the use of nuclear weapons. For this reason this volume includes the call by Dr. Fromm for unilateral steps toward nuclear disarmament which is inspired by convictions born of the nuclear dilemma rather than by absolute pacifism.

Not only are these chapters different in their conclusions concerning the problems of ethics and strategy; they also differ in their ultimate presuppositions. Three of the authors are Protestant theologians and they write against the background of their own religious tradition but they have sought to emphasize insights that can be meaningful to readers who have other orientations. On the other hand, they have not sought to disguise their frame of reference.

The question may naturally be raised: why should we separate nuclear weapons so completely from the most destructive conventional weapons used for large scale bombing in the Second World War and from such developments as bacteriological warfare which may constitute an even greater threat to humanity? I think that the answer to the first part of that question is well presented in the first two chapters, by both Dr. Herz and Dr. Inglis. As for bacteriological warfare, there is point in distinguishing nuclear warfare from the vistas of horror suggested by bacteriological warfare because our nation's policies are based upon the possession of nuclear weapons. It is one thing to experiment with methods of bacteriological warfare; but it is quite another to base national policy on the possession of nuclear weapons.

JOHN C. BENNETT

International politics
and the nuclear dilemma

BY JOHN H. HERZ

JOHN H. HERZ *is Professor of Political Science at the City College, New York. A graduate of German universities and of the Geneva Institute of International Studies, he has been connected, in teaching or research, with the Princeton Institute for Advanced Study, Trinity College (Hartford), Howard University, and, as visiting professor, with Columbia University, the New School for Social Research, and the University of California at Berkeley. He also served with the Office of Strategic Services and the State Department.*

Dr. Herz has devoted much of his study and research to the field of political theory, and, in particular, to the theory of international politics. His more general political thought is laid down in Political Realism and Political Idealism, *where he developed the theory of the "security dilemma." In* International Politics in the Atomic Age *the author investigates the impact of the new weapons upon the relationships, policies, and systems of nations.*

ONE day, in the spring of 1961, people all over the world could read that a man had for the first time circled the globe in outer space; it happened to be the same day the papers reported the beginning of the trial of another "human" being charged with the murder of six million fellow humans. The coincidence pointed up the extreme contrast between the heights of man's achievements in the material sphere and the depth of his moral failure.

The moral predicament of which the Nazi extermination camp was a symbol is now duplicated by the potentialities of thermonuclear warfare. Exactly as technology enabled the Nazis to dispose neatly, efficiently, and expeditiously of such masses of people as even a Tamerlane and other mass killers of the past had been unable to cope with, the new weapon enables us to destroy at one blow millions of lives in similarly streamlined fashion. And the moral implications of the situation are all the more vexing because the preparation is no longer based on irrational hatred or emotional ideology but on seemingly cool and rational calculation of "defense," "security," and "national interest." A decision, arrived at and implemented in bureaucratic fashion, a few minutes later and half-way around the world, "effectuates" the destruction of that part of the world; and, by way of counteraction, results in the annihilation of the "initiating" part of the world. The "transaction" as a whole produces mutual annihilation, neatly and according to plan.

This goes to show that there is not only a moral but also another, a so-to-speak physical dimension to the nuclear dilemma. Since seemingly rational action is bound to result in something utterly irrational (*mutual* annihilation, and possibly even race-suicide), the dilemma pertains to the survival of the human race in the physical sense, and therewith to all that which used to be concerned with existence, coexistence, and survival of human groups: policy. Again, contrasting the new with an older condition may serve to point up the radical novelty of our predicament. Some time ago, the newspapers reported what they referred to as "a bizarre incident": "Jet

Shot Down By Its Own Gunfire As It Speeds Faster Than Shells."[1] Substituting "mankind" for "jet," and "nuclear weapon" for "gunfire," could one have a more apt description of the potentiality inherent in our situation? Compare this with even the more pessimistic interpretations of the human condition in the past. Hobbes, for instance, saw nations, as nations, in that condition of "war of everybody against everybody" which he called the "state of nature": "In all times, Kings, and Persons of Soveraigne authority, because of their Independency, are in continuall jealousies, and in the state and posture of Gladiators; having their weapons pointing, and their eyes fixed on one another; that is, their Forts, Garrisons, and Guns, upon the Frontiers of their Kingdoms; and continuall Spyes upon their neighbors; which is a posture of War."[2] Yet he continued: "But because they uphold thereby, the Industry of their Subjects; there does not follow from it, that misery, which accompanies the Liberty of particular men."[3] Leviathan was still a protector. Hobbes understood that protection, such as there was, could only be afforded "particular men" through a "posture of war," an institution whose function it was to preserve states as units of defense and security and in this way to protect the elementary interests of their inhabitants.

This protective function of the state and its defenses seems to be in jeopardy today. The weapon has outgrown its capacity to defend. Its all-out use would not leave anything worth defending. There have been previous revolutions in weapons and arts of war that also played great havoc with traditional concepts and existing institutions (such as the gun-powder revolution). But the present revolution is unlike any earlier one in that its effects are absolute: absolute destructiveness of weapons and war; absolute penetrability of political entities; and the globe now absolutely too small for new, larger units of genuine protection. Einstein once said: "The unleashed power of the atom has changed everything except our way of thinking. Thus we are drifting toward a catastrophe beyond comparison. We shall require a substantially new manner of thinking if mankind is to survive." If we are to change our manner of thinking we must have a clear understanding of the novel phenomena and their impact. And we can hope to understand the new only when we compare it with the traditional function of weapons and war, of the state, and of international politics.

FOREIGN RELATIONS IN THE PREATOMIC AGE

What accounts for political entities—tribes, city-states, nations—their emergence and identity, their actions and their policies? There are two chief answers from opposite sides: Economic determinism, emphasizing the economic needs of people, interprets everything in the nature and the emergence of political entities in the light of economic developments; this contrasts with an interpretation which considers irrational factors like human "pride," or the aggressiveness of individuals and groups and their ensuing expansionism, as the prime causes of what happens in history.

These theories neglect the impact of weapons and defense systems. I do not propose to substitute for an economic determinism a "strategic determinism" which, in equally one-sided fashion, might consider all historical developments as superstructure on the means of destruction. But whoever studies how weapons developments and military technique have affected the structure of states and governments cannot help recognizing in how large a degree identity, structure, and interrelations of political units *are* determined by their capacity to defend themselves. This is hardly surprising. Besides the satisfaction of basic economic wants, the other most basic human need is that of protection of lives and goods; thus, the preserving of internal and external security has been a second essential function of political units. Means of defense and weapons systems determine, at least in part, what are the entities that can perform the protective function. People in the long run recognize that authority which possesses the power of protection.

One might begin with the invention of the chariot, the battle-wagon of antiquity, and its impact on the formation of ancient empire, and from there trace the connection between military technology and the emergence of political entities throughout history. For our purposes it is sufficient to follow up this relationship since the time of the emergence of the modern state and the modern state-system.

The now world-wide system of "territorial" or "nation"-states originated in Europe in the sixteenth and seventeenth centuries. Under the more primitive military conditions of the European Middle Ages units of protection could only be small: manors, castles, walled cities. Larger ones—kingdoms or similar principalities—were generally too

large for effective control. Politically this caused a muddle of overlapping, ill-defined jurisdictions into which the public power disinte-
grated under feudalism. But with the invention of gun-powder
the small medieval units became indefensible, while rulers of larger
territorial units, with the aid of standing armies, infantry, and artillery,
and backed by a rising middle class interested in a developing money
economy, were now able to free themselves from dependence on
vassals, eliminate feudal power, pacify large-scale areas, and surround
them with walls of fortifications to protect them from similarly armed
and fortified units outside. In this way, after an extended period of
transition and turmoil, the large-area, territorial state emerged as the
new unit of protection. Its nature and characteristics have largely
determined internal and international politics of the last couple of
centuries.

So much have we become used to the modern nation-state system
that we are inclined to consider its characteristics and the concepts
which relate to it as so-to-speak eternal ones, valid for all times. Closer
analysis reveals that categories like "sovereignty"and "independence,"
national interest and national power, and even "nation" itself, have all
been closely tied to the specific conditions of a particular period, emerging with these conditions and now becoming inapplicable with the
change of times and conditions. Thus, the "sovereign independence"
of the modern state simply reflected a relatively high degree of "impenetrability" of large-area territorial entities surrounded by hard
shells of military defenses that necessitated frontal attack for breach-
ing. Power, likewise, was based on the self-contained, impermeable
nature of the unit. As the sum-total of the strength of one unit relative
to others, power in the modern state-system became measurable and
calculable, and thus enabled each nation to maintain itself vis-à-vis
similar units: national power became the chief instrument of so-called
"power politics." The main features of international politics throughout
the classical period of the modern state-system were alliances, balance
of power, and limited war; and, as these terms indicate, the emerging
system, despite the absence of overruling authority, was not entirely
anarchic; in some measure, it was stable and even "conservative," in
the sense of lending itself to the preservation of the units which composed it.

It is true that, as Hobbes observed, stability of system and peace among nations might at any time be disrupted by war. This simply shows that the security dilemma in which political entities without any supranational authority or government above them necessarily find themselves was inescapable even in the classical state-system. Not knowing what the other group is up to, and compelled ultimately to rely on one's own strength for security and survival, one must be prepared for "the worst." Thus competition for power pervaded the system. Yet, under conditions of relative "impenetrability," the security dilemma could be mitigated. Small powers, which despite their "hard shells" were more easily penetrable than big ones, could join larger ones in alliances which made them, for all practical purposes, parts of larger defense systems. All could and most did see in the maintenance of a balance among all a means to prevent any one from attaining hegemony. There were indeed always those nations which were intent on destroying the system by establishing themselves as hegemony powers, from Spain in the beginning, through France, to Germany. But the system functioned in such a way that, under the leadership of a "balancer" (in modern times, England), the other major European powers would rally in time to defeat them.

War itself had a partially stabilizing function. It is true that even in this period war frequently was a force for change, too. But though it often served the aggrandizement of nations, or national unification, at other times it served as ultimate means for restoring a lost equilibrium. Indeed, major wars, or whole series of wars, can be characterized as "wars for the restoration of the balance," from the coalition wars against Louis XIV, through the "wars of liberation" against Napoleon, to World War II against Axis hegemony in the world. Without war as the ultimate means to preserve a system of self-contained, defensible entities the mitigation of power politics which the balance system implied, would not have been possible. By the twentieth century, of course, with the emergence of territorial units on the European pattern outside Europe, the European balance had become a world balance, a system in which, beginning with World War I, the United States had to relieve England in its role of the "balancer" whose intervention shifted the scales.

War was limited in other respects also. With surprisingly few exceptions, it did not serve the purpose of wiping out existing states as such. There were exceptions, such as the elimination of smaller states in wars for national unification (e.g., in Germany and Italy in the nineteenth century). But by and large the common interest in self-preservation prevailed. Under the ancient regime, the principle of legitimacy gave rulers mutually recognizing each other as rightful sovereigns an incentive not to destroy a fellow-ruler's independence, since doing so would have destroyed the very principle on which the rights of all of them rested. Subsequently, the nationality principle made it seem just as abhorrent to deprive a sovereign nation of its independence as the despoiling of a legitimate ruler had appeared before. This principle led to a proliferation of nation-states all over the world. The defensibility of many of them has now become particularly questionable. But under territoriality even a world-wide system of nationally self-determining nations would have made sense as long as they could expect to maintain their independence through the balancing process and limited war.

At a time when some degree of national security was still attainable, "national interest," that somewhat elusive indicator of foreign-policy objectives, could likewise be defined in reasonably concrete terms. Whatever more far-reaching and ambitious goals of foreign policy would from time to time be couched in terms of the national interest, it was understood to comprise at least those minimum requirements of safety which at that time could still be specified in usually concrete geographical terms: maintenance and defense of one's present territorial status and possibly, beyond the status quo, certain modest acquisitions, such as a "better" river frontier or a similar "natural" boundary. Such minimal definability of the national interest rendered even the problem of international morality manageable. True, the ancient dichotomy of individual and group ethical standards remained. Nations could not afford pacifism. Certain wars were under certain conditions meaningful and even necessary. In a way, the development of the military art, which led from the medieval feud to the territorial fortress, even meant extending the range of *raison d'Etat*. Killing human beings from a distance—abhorrent to the Middle Ages—became part of international morality, and standards of such morality, or amorality, expanded subsequently with each extension of units and range of weapons (long-range artillery, machine gun, submarine, and so forth). But as long as it was possible to distinguish minimum aims of security from more ambitious objectives of national foreign policy and as long as one could alleviate the power struggle through systems and policies like the balance of power, one could draw the line between the "moral" and the "immoral" by distinguishing between the more and the less moderate, the more and the less peaceful, the more and the less egocentered policy of nations and their rulers. International morality could be defined in the meaningful sense of giving preference to the more moderate objective and the more peaceful means if and when there was a choice. In this way, diplomacy was part not only of the rational but also of the ethical universe.

FOREIGN POLICY IN THE NUCLEAR AGE

Looking backward from our age of nuclear predicament toward the classical system of international relations, these might now appear to us as an almost idyllic interlude of protection and stability rather than the Hobbesian nightmare of war of all against all. But like every human creation it carried in itself the seeds of destruction. As early as the nineteenth century certain developments tended to inhibit the functioning of the system through their impact on that feature of the territorial state which constituted the strongest guarantee of its "sovereign independence," its hard shell of defensibility in case of war. The industrial revolution made industrialized countries dependent on the world market, so that in war, blocked off from supplies, they might now be starved into surrender. "Psychological warfare," developed primarily in our century, might likewise serve to undermine a nation's "impenetrability" through circumvention of the necessity to attack its walls of fortification frontally. But the decisive change was in the means and conduct of war itself. Air warfare already indicated the new possibility of a nation's defeat through penetration from above. And if even in World War II large-area conventional bombing did not prove quite enough to defeat a nation (breaking the fronts in East and West Europe being required in the case of Germany, and atomic weapons in that of Japan), atomic and nuclear weapons now do not seem to allow any protection against the most radical penetration. Utter permeability now negates the traditional territoriality of units, and it is exactly the most powerful nuclear powers which as targets of other nuclear powers become the most vulnerable. Utmost power coincides with utmost impotence, and the most powerful and elaborate machinery ever devised for defense and protection presages universal destruction.

Even bipolar block formation could not stay this development. The emergence, after World War II, of two huge defense systems, each comprising a large part of the globe under the leadership of one "super-power," constituted an effort to extend the principle of territoriality, now no longer applicable to the nation-state. The hard shell surrounding one single nation was simply expanded into a wall surrounding entire halves of the globe. Integrated defense systems like NATO, with troops of different block powers stationed along the rim of the block and with bases dotting its outer boundaries, are a clear expression of this purpose. Discounting the factor of nuclear exposure, a new system of large-scale area protection, defensibility, and even balance might have emerged at the end of World War II. But since the nuclear factor cannot be discounted, bipolarity merely adds to the confusion by pulling additional units into the area of permeability and possible holocaust.

Can any "sane" nuclear policy, indeed, any rational foreign policy, be developed under these circumstances? Among the numerous proponents of solutions we can distinguish those who are confident regarding what can be done without much change in the present situation from others who are pessimistic in respect to the existing condition and optimistic regarding the changes they advocate; the former want, in the main, to stabilize a status quo, the latter advocate radical change. In between are those who, realizing that change is necessary, propose to proceed gradually and by way of relatively moderate steps.

Policies of deterrence

The attitude primarily tied up with advocacy of the maintenance of the nuclear status quo is based on the emergence of what is referred to as the system of "mutual deterrence" (or "nuclear stalemate," or "balance of terror"). Since two power blocks have risen, both equipped with almost equal nuclear weapons, they can be relied upon—so this theory goes—to refrain from attacking each other for fear of retaliation. Indeed, so much reliance was placed initially upon the functioning of this system that the idea of a utopia of permanent peace was developed out of a situation of utmost peril. Churchill, at that time, believed it possible that "we would by a process of sublime irony have reached a stage in this story where safety will be the sturdy child of terror, and survival the twin-brother of annihilation."[4]

Undoubtedly, fear of nuclear retaliation has had much to do with the fact that the nuclear weapon has so far not been used. Certainly, reliance on retaliation accounts for the feeling of safety which still exists among people in many parts of the world, including the nuclear countries. But there is now much less confidence that the system will always function in this dependable way. Closer investigation of what is involved in deterrence—and the study of deterrence has by now developed into something like a special branch of the social sciences somewhere between strategy and international politics—has impressed even adherents of the status-quo attitude with the incredible complexity of the problem and thus raised serious doubts concerning too much reliance on it. Out of a welter of conflicting and often confusing views on things like "first strike" and "second strike strategy," "preventive and preemptive attack," "stable and unstable," or "symmetrical and asymmetrical deterrent situations," "counter-forces strategy," or "finite," or "graduated" deterrence, and so forth, a kind of consensus seems to emerge at least concerning what is problematical in deterrence.

Thus, there is the possibility of "war by accident," either because of somebody's "irrational" action (including the case of "nuclear war of desperation" when one side, in conventional or limited nuclear war, is about to be defeated) or, more likely, because of technical error (misinterpretation of some event, some signal, or some similarly ambiguous evidence of impending or beginning attack) or human malfunction (e.g., misinterpretation of orders, either by design or unintentionally, on the part of subordinates). Ever shorter time available between discovery of a suspicious phenomenon and decision, and ever greater spread of retaliatory installations and weapons must obviously add to these dangers.

Even besides accidental war there remains enough uncertainty in mutual deterrence. Stable deterrence means absence of decisive technological "breakthroughs"; how can they be prevented without strict supervision? And even under conditions of stability where each side has about what the opponent has, a temptation may well develop to strike first and destroy the opponent by "surprise attack"; it depends on one's calculation of the risks involved. If one side believes that, by striking first, it can destroy so much of the opponent's retaliatory force that the damage to be expected in retaliation is not unacceptable, it will sooner or later justify such a policy by claiming that it owes it to history or its "cause" once and for all to wipe capitalist imperialism from the face of the earth; or, conversely, that it cannot afford to miss the chance to rid the world once and for all of the scourge of Communism. The security dilemma itself, which reaches its pinnacle in the nuclear situation, reinforces such temptations. Not knowing whether the opponent is not calculating exactly as outlined above, one may be driven to forestall his presumed "preventive" blow by one's own "preventive" blow—a first strike to avert a first strike. Somebody will always be able to prove that "this is the last chance" either because of one's present margin of superiority (which may vanish) or because of one's inferiority (which may tempt the opponent to strike first).

A further serious hazard in mutual deterrence is misunderstanding concerning the *casus belli nuclearis;* that is, "war by miscalculation" may break out because the circumstances are left undefined or unclear in which "aggression" or a similarly provocative step on the part of one side will cause the other side to react by nuclear force; for instance, where "massive" nuclear retaliation is being threatened in case of "serious" aggression. While the uncertainty inherent in such a threat may well cause the other side to abstain from aggressive or expansionist moves in 99 out of 100 cases, it may be misled into action in the 100th instance where it mistakenly believes that no nuclear retaliation will be forthcoming. True, a policy of spelling out exactly when "massive retaliation" may be expected has its disadvantages too; it would by implication define cases and areas to which the retaliatory threat would not apply, this way encouraging attack there. It has been suggested that a mutual commitment not under any circumstances to use all-out nuclear weapons first would eliminate such uncertainties; it would further eliminate the use of "nuclear blackmail" to attain one's ends. But while this would pretty well eliminate the danger of war by miscalculation, it would put that side at a disadvantage which is inferior in conventional armaments, which at this point means the West. Such a commitment on the part of the West would therefore have to be coupled with an effort to achieve a better balance of conventional forces, which, in the absence of arms control reducing the East to some equilibrium level, implies Western rearmament, e.g., of NATO forces in Europe. Conventional rearmament has become necessary in any event—even apart from a "no first strike" commitment—since the threat of American nuclear retaliation in case of Soviet attack with conventional weapons on allies has become less plausible now that American cities are within reach of Soviet missiles. *Si vis pacem, para bellum non-atomicum.* Only in this way can an ultimate situation where one might be faced with the agonizing choice between starting the holocaust and surrendering be avoided or, at least, be made less likely.

In the face of these difficulties it has been suggested that both sides aim at making the deterrence system more stable by rendering the deterrent force invulnerable. Instead of chasing after nuclear "superiority" through developing ever more weapons of ever more destructive force—something nonsensical in an age of nuclear plenty where an opponent, even though inferior in absolute number of weapons, has in any event enough for saturation—the existing weapons system should be protected in such a way that no attack can wipe it out; that is, it should be rendered invulnerable through "hardening" missile bases or through dispersal, mobility, or concealment of weapons and delivery systems. Thus, ability to survive any first strike and come back with devastating effect would seem to provide an absolute guarantee that a first strike will never be undertaken.

Apart from the question whether absolute invulnerability is obtainable, doubts arise even here. The risk of war by accident is not diminished (perhaps, through dispersal, etc., even increased). Temptation to stage preventive or surprise attack may be reduced. But an attack, conventional or even nuclear, on *non*-nuclear powers may even be encouraged where there is no longer any assurance of retaliation by invulnerable nuclear powers on their behalf. This lack of protection may drive more and more powers to develop their own nuclear deterrent, as in the case of France. Ironically, then, increased stability between two powers might give rise to complete instability in a system of plural nuclear powers. The world may become one of an indefinite, growing number of independent nuclear power centers.

Such an extension of the "nuclear club" (the so-called "n'th power" problem) represents a grave danger to the system of mutual deterrence. While the acquisition of nuclear weapons might give the new nuclear powers some amount of protection against nuclear blackmail, it also means that, where today some measure of rational calculation is still possible among what in essence amounts to two, and only two, clearcut opponents, an indefinite number of non-aligned powers would bring about an indefinite and infinite extension of risks of error, of action in madness, or in despair, or out of spite, or for reasons of domestic policy, or—especially in the case of conflicts between smaller powers—for the sake of local or regional policy. Such nuclear polycentrism imaginably even renders the attacker unidentifiable, giving an anonymous aggressor a chance to instigate nuclear contest among others ("catalytic war," as it has been called).

Even now, with only two power centers, the complex nature of the considerations and calculations involved in the deterrent situation constitutes perhaps the most unstabilizing factor of all. Deterrence becomes dependent on a "complicated process of mutual mind-reading," upon the credibility of threats and similar policies.[5] Where policy previously was based on the relatively simple assessment of military capabilities, it now becomes the result of assessment and counter-assessment of attitudes and intentions.* And where previously, if the worst came to the worst, malassessment might mean outbreak of and defeat in war, its consequence now may be an infinitely greater disaster: mutual annihilation. For, it is the most paradoxical effect of nuclear penetrability that the weapon is successful only as long as it remains an unused threat; used, it means deadly failure.

The difficulty is compounded by the fact that whatever calculations and assessments seem rational may be too complex to be explicable to the public at large which, at least in democracies, where public opinion counts in policy and strategic planning, must have a minimum understanding of attitudes and preparations—too complex, maybe, even for the policy-makers themselves. How then can these calculations become the basis of policy? For these reasons it has even been suggested that retaliatory reaction should be made completely automatic so that the retaliatory blow would be released by machine rather than by the conscious decision of a leader. It needs hardly to be pointed out that, while nuclear blackmail or war caused by miscalculation of the opponent's reaction to one's own actions may be avoided in this way, the danger of war by accident would increase immeasurably.

---

* One is reminded of a Jewish story from old Russia. Shmule meets Moshe on the road and asks him, "Where do you go?" Moshe: "To Minsk." Shmule: "When you say 'I go to Minsk,' you want me to believe that you go to Pinsk, but I know that you go to Minsk, so why do you lie?"

Advocacy of radical change

In the face of the doubts and difficulties involved in policies of deterrence, must we then despair, or resign ourselves to a fate from which there is no escape? It is understandable that some of the solutions advocated by those favoring a radical change in present policies are based on a feeling of despair. Confronting the alternative of "rather dead than Red," or "rather Red than dead," it might, under nuclear conditions, not be mere cowardice to opt for the latter and give up liberty so that mankind can at least continue to exist. While in times past the heroic self-sacrifice of individuals or groups for the sake of their ideals was meaningful, it is questionable whether the present generation would have the right, by sacrificing itself, to doom perhaps all future generations as well. Capitulation, so one might feel, would at least leave the hope that the victorious system like all systems and regimes before, would in time be transformed or pass away.

It is this alternative and this choice which is implied in the propositions of the "unilateralists," those who propose either nuclear or total unilateral disarmament. An expectation, sometimes voiced, that this would shame the other side into following one's own example seems illusory. Communist leaders who, on the basis of their doctrine, might well be convinced that the abdication merely proved Western degeneracy, are not likely to be so influenced even by "world opinion." True, the idea, sometimes proferred by those who object to unilateralism, that the Soviets would then drop the "Bomb" right away or force immediate surrender by threatening to do so, is over-simplified. More likely they would use the next international crisis to extend their power.

The radicalism of unilateralism supposes that there is no choice. If there really were no alternative to launching the nuclear holocaust or capitulation, we would indeed confront an agonizing situation. But it seems that, if some advocates of deterrence have sinned through over-optimism, this approach sins through over-pessimism. At least today, other choices are still open. Even among the advocates of radical change some put their hopes in such possibilities. There are the world federalists who believe that nothing short of world government can and will solve the nuclear dilemma. It is certainly in the logic of weapons developments that only global authority could henceforth provide the protection which no partial power or block, however large and "powerful," can convey any longer. But to infer that what "ought to be" or "must be" "will happen" is pseudo-logic. How to get from a situation of extreme power-concentration in separate power units to world authority in one jump is not apparent. Could it perhaps be done by disarmament (general, not unilateral), as proposed by other "radicals"?

The story of the efforts to achieve universal disarmament, now again on the agenda through Khrushchev's proposal, is the long and sad saga of failure—failure not only in regard to practical, diplomatic attempts to arrive at agreement—which would not be conclusive in view of the urgency, under nuclear conditions, to try again and again—but more seriously because of theoretical objections. No plausible plan can disregard the need for internal "police" forces and armament to cope with domestic disorder. Even if these could be fixed in such a way as not to give anybody international advantage, the status of external defenselessness which would ensue would seem to put too high a premium on deception. Suppose that an agreement on controlled armament allows each side a maximum of 500 nuclear weapons; if one side hides 50 more, the balance would not thereby be fatally disturbed. But in an environment of supposedly complete disarmament such cheating would convey overwhelming superiority on the evader. Under "complete disarmament," therefore, it is likely that nobody would be able to resist the urge to evade and conceal, if merely for reasons of security, and the ensuing uncertainties and suspicions might render conditions more unstable than they would be at higher armament levels. These considerations also apply to mere nuclear disarmament. In either case, safe controls through "ironclad inspection" would be necessary to overcome evasion, and such controls are impossible, even for nuclear stockpiles. Ironically enough, both the believers in mutual deterrence and the believers in disarmament are in a sense eighteenth-century optimists: The former because they put all stock in rational behavior, the latter because they must make everything dependent on "fair play."

The picture we derive from an analysis of both the "status quo" and the "radical" schools is grim. There are, however, proposals of a third group of analysts envisaging less radical, more moderate and gradual changes. It is probably somewhere in-between the "standpat" attitudes of the preparedness crowd and the visionary utopianism of the radicals that progress toward heightened security and lessened tension can realistically be expected.

What can be done?

Many limited proposals have been made in the field of armaments proper. Whatever their nature, one should begin where *some* control, *some* regulation seems possible. Since the dawn of the atomic age opportunities have tragically been missed time and again simply by allowing that moment to pass when certain steps were still technically feasible. Thus control of production or stockpiling of atomic bombs, at first possible, became impossible with the passing of time. If today the use of outer space for military purposes can still be prevented by agreements on inspection and similar control measures, this may no longer be possible tomorrow or next year. If it is still possible to halt the spread of nuclear armaments to non-nuclear countries, it may soon be too late. Agreement on cessation of nuclear tests has long been deferred; what is clearly controllable there should be controlled. But there are pitfalls even in matters of moderate arms control. There is not only the general difficulty of preventing evasion but also the little discussed problem of enforcement. What should be the penalty for discovered evasion? If all that can be done is to permit the "cheated" to do what the cheater clandestinely has begun before, he may be at a great disadvantage, and such an "asymmetry" might itself encourage evasion. And there is irony as well as danger in the fact that inspection systems, surveillance measures, etc., may themselves create those suspicions and increase those tensions they were supposed to alleviate; thus, conflict over discovery of some slight or alleged evasion may conceivably lead to a crisis where non-discovery might have produced less dangerous consequences.

Therefore, that which can be done unilaterally or by tacit agreement may occasionally be less risky than formal control systems. Nuclear powers intent on not misleading the opponent into precipitate action should plan their policies carefully so as to avoid anything which could be provocative, even though intended defensively, like "fail-safe" test flights toward "enemy" territory. They should make sure that communication remains possible and open with the opponent during periods of tension, and even after hostilities have occurred.

They might disperse their industries and emphasize and strengthen meaningful civil defense, not only in the interest of actual protection of the population but also in order to make their defensive nuclear policy more plausible. These are ways to render deterrence more stable, wars less likely, perhaps even hostilities more limited.

One of the main suggestions in this area concerns "limited war," and in particular limited nuclear war. There is certainly great merit in trying to devise policies under which even nuclear war would be "tamed." The more enthusiastic supporters of the idea assert that, through use of smaller and "cleaner" weapons and dispersal of task forces, such a war would turn out to be even less destructive than was conventional war just prior to the atomic age. But this seems doubtful, especially since limited nuclear war is least likely to occur in sparsely populated jungle regions and similar out-of-the-way parts of the world; it is most likely to occur in populous industrial regions such as Western Europe where it would be so devastating as to become indistinguishable from all-out war to the peoples affected. Besides, there is always the danger of "escalation," of limited war gradually but irresistibly snowballing into all-out war. Indeed, this problem also presents itself in the case of conventional war; for, once general hostilities involve major powers, the use of first limited and ultimately unlimited nuclear weapons will tempt belligerents as long as they possess them as "deterrents."

The impact of the new weapon is most directly noticeable in the field of military strategy, but it is no less decisive in foreign policy where weapons and war used to be the *ultima ratio*. Where "mere" conventional war now involves a threat of ultimate catastrophe, war seems to be available to policy only as bluff; even then it is tremendously dangerous, since the bluffing game may fail when nobody knows who's bluffing whom. On the other hand, what means of policy exist where force is no longer available? How can powers then pursue their objectives?

It is clear that in the field of policy, as in that of strategy, more "radical" proposals become increasingly doubtful. It is in a way understandable that the threat which Communism poses to a "free world" induces some to advocate "getting it over with" at one blow, either in the world at large or in specific regions where Communism installs itself; or to emphasize "preparedness" to the exclusion of any kind of negotiation or accommodation. But the seriousness of this threat to the West is matched by the threat of the weapon to all mankind. Not only can we no longer indulge in "wars of liberation"; even the traditional "war for the restoration of the balance of power" is now implausible. Not only must we ourselves refrain from force, we must do all we can to prevent the opponent from resorting to something which would be suicidal to all. The nuclear predicament challenges statesmen to act in a dual capacity: not only in defense of "national" interest but as agents and caretakers of what Reinhold Niebuhr calls the developing "community of the fate of the common threat of nuclear annihilation." A new realism of universalism must put the common weal—in the elementary sense of a common interest in survival—before the traditional interest in having one's opponent commit mistakes. The great religions and moral systems of the world have exalted an altruistic behavior-pattern, according to which consideration was given to the interests of others, whether individuals or nations. Under the standards of a new humanism which places the preservation of the human race above any and all partial interests, the same behavior-pattern now emerges as indispensable to national policy if the entire race is not to perish.

Most important among the emerging more moderate foreign policy attitudes are therefore those which stress the necessity of maintaining a balance between the two major blocks and systems. This seems to involve a policy of mutual accommodation, of delimitation of spheres, by and large on the basis of the bipolar status quo. Such an approach could not fail to reduce suspicions and relax tensions; nuclear war, except accidental war, will hardly break out without "war crises." It might also create an environment where those moderate and realizable arms agreements which we have mentioned would have a better chance of success, for armaments problems cannot be separated from the general political climate. It is true that acceptance of the present status would involve renunciations and sacrifices of broader aims on either side. But the recognitions involved would not have to sanction regimes or territorial acquisitions in any moral sense; they would merely constitute the practical acknowledgement of what exists *de facto,* and the renunciation of claims to what, being under the opponent's control, could in any event be gotten only by force. It could, on the other hand, eliminate dangerous trouble spots. If a firmer guarantee of West Berlin and the access routes could be obtained through Western recognition of the Oder-Neisse line and the East German regime, or if a confirmation of the present status of Taiwan was obtainable in return for recognition of the Peiping regime as *de facto* government of the Chinese mainland, this might appear worth the price. And so around the world. This delimitation of spheres would not, by itself, solve the problem of indirect penetration into the other side's sphere, through economic means, political infiltration, or "subversion." Here, and especially in the intermediate world of "uncommitted" and underdeveloped nations, the West must accept the Communist challenge to "peaceful competition," and it can do so if it trusts its economic means and the power and impact of its political and general ideals, provided it is ready to make the necessary sacrifices, financial and otherwise. Force has always been a poor response to the challenge of revolutionary or even pseudo-revolutionary movements anyway. There certainly is great risk for the West in Communist dynamism. Still, the danger to us and all would be immeasurably greater if the Chinese doctrine of the "inevitable war" should prevail over present Soviet realization of war's suicidal nature. A Chinese leader is said to have suggested that such a war might spare ten million Americans, 20 million Russians, and 300 million Chinese. The implications of such an attitude are terrifying. As in the field of armaments proper, it would be tragic if the chances of negotiating a political rapprochement with a relatively moderate opponent were allowed to pass. Ever so slight actual successes (the neutralization of Austria, the agreement to keep Antarctica demilitarized) point out the direction in which to go.

Paradoxes in the nuclear situation

Nothing will be easy or easily gained in an approach of this nature. It is much easier to continue habitual policies of the national interest narrowly conceived. But in that case a catastrophic blowup will become an almost mathematical certainty. On the other hand, we must be aware of the paradoxes which confront the attitudes here considered. The paradoxes are in the things themselves, and it is therefore not surprising that they are reflected in attitudes and policies. How shall one act consistently and rationally in a world where utmost power coincides with impotence, where power of protection, based on armaments of unimaginable potency, vanishes because the weapons are not to be used, where, in other words, the familiar unit of security no longer fulfils its function of affording security? In such a situation, everything is driven to its ultimate: What is most urgently needed is also the most hazardous and dangerous. If we try to develop an "absolute" weapon (such as missiles fired from undiscoverable submarines) in order to have an "absolutely" stable deterrent, we also run the danger that should it ever fail in its deterrent effect it would prove to be the most absolutely destructive. If in the present nuclear situation a show of absolute determination to resist and retaliate is necessary to avoid giving the impression of bluffing, this will, if it fails to deter, lead to all-out war or else a loss of face equalling surrender. The element of uncertainty in leaving the *casus belli* indefinite may successfully deter, but if it ever causes one side to misinterpret the other's intentions, it means war by miscalculation; this was the case in Korea, and today the chances of general blowup would be much larger.

Similarly, an effective civil defense system which would give plausible evidence of a determination to retaliate (and thereby increase the chances of deterrence and security from war) would be utterly destructive of our "way of life":

> The new developments will cause people to burrow more deeply into the ground. Factories will be built in caves, as will apartment houses and stores. Eventually most human life will be underground, confronted by arsenals capable of destroying all life over the land areas of the earth.[6]

These paradoxes are reflected in language itself, which here, as often, betrays underlying traits and trends. The new language of the nuclear age indicates that weapons (machines) take the place of humans; human relations are "reified," machine relations "humanized." We speak of "second generations" of weapons, not people; of their "overkill capacity"; of the "survivability" of weapons systems; of "invulnerability" again of armaments, not men.

The paradoxes recur in the contradictory advice of experts, where both sides seem often equally convincing. Thus, the arguments of the erudite for or against limited nuclear war are about equally strong on either side; or consider a more recent debate on the merits of making NATO a separate, fourth nuclear power.[7] Little wonder, then, that policies get confused again and again, even where serious efforts are being made to solve previously mixed-up issues. Thus, in the all-important area of the "first or second strike" problem, President Kennedy, in one and the same message on defense problems, managed to straddle the issue by advocating both mutually exclusive policies. The message began with an emphasis on America's second-strike policy: United States strategic defenses must make it clear to the potential aggressor "that sufficient retaliatory forces will be able to revive after a first strike. . . . *We will not strike first in any conflict.* But what we must have is the ability to survive a first blow and respond with devastating power." Later, it asserted the necessity of striking first in certain circumstances: "In the event of a major aggression that could not be repulsed by conventional forces we must be prepared to take *whatever action with whatever weapons are appropriate.*" "Major aggression" obviously refers to non-nuclear aggressions too, and thus first-strike policy is envisaged here. In the end, the President reverted to his initial, second-strike posture: "As a power which will never strike first, our hopes for anything close to an absolute deterrent must rest on weapons which rest on hidden, movable, or invulnerable bases. . . ."[8]

Perhaps this reflects the travails of a still inexperienced administration. Somewhat the same kind of confusion has been noticeable in the more "political" sector of American foreign policy, where attempts at preparing the ground for an apparently broad and comprehensive effort at accommodation are hampered by a kind of "nineteenth century"-type approach to more specific problems, like Cuba. Neither East nor West, nor anyone else, can any longer afford policies of "going it alone," of national security in the old-fashioned sense. The necessity of a long-range, consistent policy line, indeed, of a new philosophy of foreign policy, imposes itself when one considers world trends and world problems not only in the area of nuclear strategy and bipolar block policy but also in other fields. This is not the place to discuss in any detail the other world revolutions of our time and the problems they raise. But it is important to realize that there, too, we encounter similar difficulties and even paradoxes. There is the sweep toward "One World"; for the first time in the history of civilizations one of them, the Western, has become world-wide, rendering the world "one" at least in a technical sense. At the same time, with the awakening of the colored races, with their very entrance into a technologically unified world, "one world" is breaking apart into ever more national entities; and while nationalism and national entities can no longer fulfil their once basic function, nationalist sentiment seems to be the mainstay of the emerging peoples of the world. Somehow their increasing number must be fitted into a world of "peaceful coexistence."

Another paradox concerns the "population explosion," not of nations but of human beings. While technological developments for the first time in history indicate a chance that mankind may live in plenty as far as its material wants are concerned, the increase in the world's population is such that it threatens to cancel out all benefit of increased production, so that the very subsistence of mankind in the material sense seems now threatened.

And in the field of belief-systems, where ideologies and their propagation poison the international atmosphere like fall-out poisoning the air, people and nations still feel that they are committed to certain values which they cannot sacrifice without giving up their "way of life." At the same time, the two most important systems with contrasting ideologies tend to become more similar to each other in many respects, and especially in their organization and structure as large-scale industrial mass societies. While to some, in particular to the intellectuals, it still makes all the difference in the world whether they live on this or the other side of the Iron Curtain, to the New York, London, or Moscow straphanger it seems to make less of a difference. At a time when the development of personality, or "the dignity of man," appears as the highest goal, trends in the organization of the economy, of culture and entertainment, and even in government and politics, threaten to render the individual a cog in the machine, while strategic developments leave him an even more insignificant, tiny unit of protection, or destruction; that is, unless he belongs to those few who have today more actual control over the fate of billions than leaders ever possessed before.

The ethics of universalism

In all this confusion one can yet discern trends and directions which policy might follow. The world has become surveyable, and world-wide planning of policy has become possible. If we take the population problem, for instance, a consistent, long-range policy based upon world-consciousness can pay attention to the effect policies of foreign aid and development have in this area; it might therefore establish priorities, under which preference would be given to nations that promise to tackle not only such problems as that of their land tenure, but also that of their population pressures, since without the solution of the latter problem everything else seems to be futile. So also in regard to problems of exhaustion of soil and other resources. Such truly conservative and preservative policy would in the long run even pay political and security dividends to the policy-inaugurating countries, since it would lead to the establishment of sounder, more viable national entities less likely to fall victims to Communist infection.

In the field of ideologies, a policy of the common interest might well identify and take into consideration those fundamental value-standards of the respective opponent which in the process of accommodation and "give and take" he cannot be supposed to sacrifice, exactly as one would oneself refuse concessions in matters of principle. Thus, while the West could not permit populations now free and to whose freedom it has committed itself to pass under Communist control (West Berlin comes to mind), Communists might find it similarly impossible to yield to "capitalism" what to them constitutes "socialist achievements" (East Germany, perhaps, is a case in point). Such distinction between the negotiable and the non-negotiable would by itself serve to clear the air and reduce tensions created by unfulfillable claim, threat, and recrimination. It is in between such opposite value-standards that policy, in our age, will have to find its tortuous way.

It is at this point, perhaps, that the difference between the traditional policy of the "national interest" and the new, world-conscious approach reveals itself most clearly. As we have seen, so long as weapons were less destructive and wars limited, the basic security interests of nations could be spelled out in concrete terms, and one could even establish minimum precepts of "international morality" on this basis. Today, distinguishing between more or less "moderate" policies in regard to the security of individual nations hardly makes sense anymore. Absolute permeability renders even the more powerful nations insecure unless they control the world. Geographic proximity of "enemy" territory or bases makes less and less of a difference where the delivery time of missiles is measured in minutes. Where distance no longer matters and a nation's security may be threatened from anywhere on the globe, it no longer makes sense to judge the "morality" of a foreign policy on the basis of whether its objectives and concerns are more or less limited, or more or less ambitious geographically.*

If distinguishing between policies by ethical yardsticks is to make sense, it must henceforth be founded on different grounds. These grounds are found in what can be established as "common interests of mankind": Its interest in physical survival, that is, avoidance of all-out war; its interest in rational planning of populations, resources, development of the under-developed; its emerging new common domain in outer space, and so forth. As pointed out before, this approach implies that the statesman now act in the dual capacity of caretaker of his own unit's as well as the larger community's interests. If such a policy of taking into consideration, together with one's own, the interest of the world at large and even the opponent's, should lead to an extended period of relaxation of tension, one might then perhaps envisage a future where more radically new attitudes would gradually replace concern with national interests. This then would constitute the international ethics of the nuclear age. I have called this approach a "universalist" one and defined universalism as "that comprehension of mankind as one group which imposes itself on those aware of the absolute peril in which the new weapons have placed mankind."⁹

If one considers this peril, on the one hand, and the manifold "one world" trends, on the other, such an approach can hardly be called entirely unrealistic. Prior to our age of radical novelty, it is true, advocacy of policies substituting the observance of universal interests for national interests was considered utopian, and correctly so, because national interests could only be safeguarded by nation-states as units of power and protection, while most internationalist ideals ran counter to what nations could afford. Now the former dichotomy of interests and ideals has changed into two opposed sets of interests, with the former ideal constituting a compelling interest itself. In preatomic times the lives of people, their goods and possessions, their hopes and

---

* Secretary of State Dean Rusk has expressed this neatly: "If you don't pay attention to the periphery, the periphery changes. And the first thing you know the periphery is the center. . . . Peace and security are world-wide." (Transcript of news conference, *The New York Times,* May 5, 1961.)

their happiness were tied up with the affairs of the country in which they lived and which protected them. Now that destruction threatens everybody in every single one of his most intimate, personal interests, national interests are bound to compete with and eventually to recede behind the common interest in sheer survival. If we add to this the general interest in the solution of the other great world problems, it is perhaps permissible to concede at least some chance to the ultimate spread of an attitude through which rational foreign policies would at last become possible.

NOTES

1. *The New York Times,* October 10, 1956.
2. Leviathan, I, chapter 13.
3. *ibid.*
4. Speech in the House of Commons, March 1, 1955.
5. Robert E. Osgood, "Stabilizing the Military Environment," *American Political Science Review,* 55 (1), March 1961, p. 25.
6. Harrison Brown and James Real, *Community of Fear,* Center for the Study of Democratic Institutions, Santa Barbara, Calif., 1960, p. 38.
7. Pro: Henry A. Kissinger, *The Necessity for Choice,* New York, 1960, pp. 121 ff., and "For an Atlantic Confederacy," *The Reporter,* February 2, 1961, pp. 16ff.; contra: Albert Wohlstetter, "Nuclear Sharing: NATO and the N+1 Country," *Foreign Affairs,* 39 (3), April 1961, pp. 355ff. (especially 372ff.).
8. From President Kennedy's message on defense spending, quoted from *The New York Times,* March 29, 1961 (emphasis supplied).
9. *International Politics in the Atomic Age* (New York, 1959), p. 309.

The nature of nuclear war

BY DAVID RITTENHOUSE INGLIS

DAVID R. INGLIS *is a Senior Physicist at the Argonne National Laboratory, Illinois, where for the last twelve years he has been engaged primarily in theoretical investigations of the structure of the nucleus. His teaching and research as Associate Professor at Johns Hopkins University was interrupted by World War II, during which he spent three years at Los Alamos in the effort which produced the first atomic bomb. In 1955-56 he taught at the University of California at Berkeley, and in 1957-58 worked at the European International Physics Laboratory, CERN, at Geneva. From 1959-60 he served as Chairman of the Federation of American Scientists.*

Since before the first atomic explosion at Alamagordo, Dr. Inglis has been concerned about how a stable world could be constructed in the face of the threat of atomic destruction. A frequent writer on disarmament and related questions, in 1951 he first started urging the establishment of a national agency to explore these problems far in advance of negotiation and three years later he made the first public proposal of a nuclear test-ban agreement as a means of limiting the further development of weapons.

Our concepts of civilization, of political institutions, of religion and morality, and of war have all grown up together, gradually, throughout history and before. Suddenly in the middle twentieth century, one of them, the concept of war, has radically changed. Nuclear sources of devastating energy, the A-bomb and the H-bomb, have suddenly multiplied by a million the power of the weapons which can be used by man. The word "war," to which we have become accustomed in the past, is no longer adequate to describe what we can expect, but we have no better word. We can call it "nuclear war," and we must learn to feel how very different nuclear war is likely to be from the wars with chemical explosives which mankind has survived in the past.

Wars with stone weapons between tribes, wars between city states or wars of expanding empires with sword and spear or musket, wars within states over political principle, and the two World Wars with massed surface warfare and aerial delivery of chemical high explosives have almost all involved comparatively small parts of the populace of a large region in direct conflict at any one time. Devastation has struck one place then another at such a slow pace that partial recovery, with succour from less disorganized regions, has been possible before the next blow. The invasion of Persia by Ghengis Khan was a classic exception, when the superior military organization of a large nation made possible such complete devastation that Persia never really recovered from it, but this was just one country among many in the medieval world. Such exceptions were few partly because mass extermination of a population was hard work in those days, requiring a lot of muscle behind the sword. The great new fact with which we must now contend is that mass extermination has become sickeningly easy and cheap in the nuclear age.

We have been wont to draw our most profound wisdom from the past, to put great faith in learning the lessons of history. If the simple lesson of history teaches us anything in this completely new situation, it is that, since there always have been wars, there always will be. Yet the prospective dimensions of nuclear war are so alarming that there must be no more large-scale war. The imagination of man, which has unlocked the atom for better or for worse, must find a way to put a sudden stop to the historic succession of large-scale wars. Before we can bring ourselves to put aside our historic ways of thinking, before we can unleash the imagination of man to cope with the problem, we must not only understand but "feel in our bones" the new dimensions of nuclear war.

Whereas, with the limited destructiveness of wars of the past, there has always been the prospect of a possible profitable outcome from war, understanding of the new dimensions of war will convince rational leaders that this is no longer so. Herein lies the hope that, with sufficient imagination, a way can be found to exploit the mutual interest of all nations to avoid nuclear war, an interest so vital when properly understood that it should transcend in importance all conflicting interests of the nations.

In a world beset with conflicting ideologies and a population explosion, the challenge to the designers of a satisfactory solution is great indeed. The task is not easy. Yet the amount of creative research and inventiveness that has been devoted to this problem is small compared to what has been expended on some other fields, such as the development of nuclear weapons.

THE POWER OF ONE BOMB

Much of the destruction of World War II was caused by bombs of about one ton of TNT. Later in the war we heard of the development of the big "blockbuster," which contained about ten tons of TNT. These, we learned, packed a terrific wallop, destroyed several buildings and indeed knocked out practically a whole city block at once. The very biggest ones contained almost twenty tons of TNT. The first primitive "firecracker" of the atomic age, which exploded over Hiroshima, had a thousand times as much power as that, twenty kilotons. A big H-bomb has another thousand times as much power as the Hiroshima bomb, a million times as much as a big "blockbuster."

It's hard to understand a factor of a million. Perhaps the housewife should contemplate her job of feeding three or four hungry mouths of a family, then imagine the job of feeding a big city of three or four million people, like Philadelphia or Chicago. Think of taking a week to drive up and down all the streets at 20 miles an hour just to catch a glimpse of all their houses!

For anyone who has read some description of the devastation which took place in Rotterdam or Hamburg or London or Cologne or Coventry or Tokyo or any of the dozens of cities which suffered enormous and tragic and irreparable losses from chemical explosives in World War II, perhaps the best way to try to imagine the power of one big H-bomb is to think of all this destructive power dumped on one city in the flash of one single explosion. That is just part of what one H-bomb can do. One single twenty-megaton H-bomb delivers more explosive power than that of all the weapons used by all nations for all purposes during all the years of World War II, or, for that matter, during all the wars of history.

Those big TNT bombs destroyed mainly by means of blast, by the sudden wave of air pressure which is capable of knocking over walls and flattening the surroundings. Special smaller bombs were also used for shrapnel and for setting fires. Besides its enormous blast effect, a nuclear bomb also destroys by radiation, which is completely different from anything known in TNT bombs. The radiation effects are of two main kinds, instantaneous and lingering.

The instantaneous radiation consists of gamma-rays and neutrons which have harmful biological effects, and of heat and light rays that can cause severe skin burns and can set fire to buildings and trees far beyond the region of heavy blast damage.

The lingering radiation has its damaging effect through fallout. The nuclear disintegrations which give power to the bomb give rise to radioactive products, substances which give off harmful radiations the way radium does for quite a long time after their formation. The burst makes a large "ball of fire" perhaps several miles in diameter full of a high density of all kinds of radiation. If this ball of fire contacts the ground, as it will in most cases, the neutrons and other radiations make the materials of the ground radioactive, too, while the heat vaporizes them. These materials are added to the radioactive materials from the bomb itself to make the great radioactive cloud that forms in the enormous rising column of hot air from the bomb.

The most intensely radioactive materials retain their potency for only a few hours or days; the somewhat less intense but still very dangerously radioactive sources last for weeks or years. What goes up must come down, and when it does, it is called "fallout." The most dangerous part of the fallout is that which comes down soonest, consisting of the larger dust particles, contaminating with dangerous radiation a great strip of land downwind from the explosion. Six hours after the explosion of a moderate-sized one-megaton H-bomb, the strip in which there is enough radiation to be surely lethal to those exposed is ten to twenty miles wide and extends about 75 miles downwind. At eighteen hours, it extends about 120 miles downwind, and the regions of very harmful and perhaps lethal radiation extend much further at later times. After a test of a larger H-bomb at Bikini, there were several injuries and one death due to the exposure of the small crew of a Japanese fishing trawler well over a thousand miles away. While this event illustrates the danger, it is not typical of what we should expect from the use of H-bombs on land areas. Without a good underground shelter, it is worse to be on land than on a boat because a person above ground, in a house, for example, receives radiation from the fallout materials settled on the broad expanse of nearby land. The Japanese fishermen could have saved themselves by washing themselves and swabbing the deck, but on land it is necessary either to have extremely thick walls (much thicker than those of a brick house) or to go below ground level for protection from the fallout, and to stay there for weeks.

We have, of course, heard a great deal about fallout in connection with nuclear testing programs in peace time, because that is the part of bomb effects which cannot always be confined to a remote test area. The more localized effects of blast and the immediate radiation are capable of inflicting the more serious damage if an H-bomb is used in war. The grim combination of an enormously powerful blast crushing buildings and the thermal radiation setting them afire after they have been reduced to tinder constitutes the most serious threat. For a one-megaton bomb, the crushing effect of the blast reaches three or four miles (three for brick apartments and four for frame houses), and for a large H-bomb, one of ten megatons, this range is seven to nine miles.

Almost everyone caught within this radius (all but perhaps a few near the edges) will be killed either by the collapse of buildings or by suffocation in the subsequent firestorm. When many buildings are set afire simultaneously throughout a large area in which the buildings are close together, as they are in cities, the result is like a gigantic bonfire. The rising column of hot air at the center makes a strong wind blowing inward which whips up the flames and spreads them from house to house, until everything is ablaze in a searing heat and there is no air to breathe.

The problem of providing protective shelters for this region is so difficult as to be usually considered hopeless. Within a quarter of a mile of the center, a big bomb can create a crater a couple of hundred feet deep and would crush or vaporize any shelter less deep than that. Beyond this inner zone, a deep shelter would provide protection against blast and radiation, but the need for air to breathe during the firestorm would require expensive preparations. With warning times of a few minutes, it is doubtful that people could be gotten into shelters in time anyway.

The fire-storm area is quite sure to encompass the part of a city strongly damaged by blast, because the crushing of buildings removes the protection of brick walls, exposes broken timbers, and facilitates the setting and spreading of fires. This is a circle three to nine miles in radius (six to eighteen miles in diameter), depending on the size of H-bomb and type of structure, as already stated. The firestorm may extend much further, for the distance at which the flash can kindle easily combustible materials is about three times as far as that. In this zone beyond very heavy blast damage, serious skin burns from the heat flash will be a source of severe suffering among those who survive the blast and fires.

Besides the blast and the heat flash, there is another localized type of damage from the instantaneous nuclear radiation. However, for H-bombs this is not very important because it is effective only about two miles out, and would merely give radiation sickness that would cause death in a few hours or days to people who would anyhow be killed in a few seconds or minutes by blast and fire. For smaller nuclear weapons, the blast is reduced more than is the nuclear radiation and the latter may inflict extensive injury as was the case at Hiroshima and Nagasaki.

In this grim business of anticipating damage from a single H-bomb, one draws circles in quite an impersonal way to show where certain types of damage are expected. Then one gives impersonal numbers to represent the number of anticipated casualties within these circles, the number of people killed and the number maimed, and the numbers are very large. When dealing with numbers too large for us to really comprehend them, we use abbreviations or nicknames. When the A-bomb turned out to be so much more powerful than a chemical bomb, the name kiloton was introduced, the power of a thousand tons of the standard chemical explosive, TNT. When the H-bomb came along, a larger unit was needed, the megaton, the power of a million tons of TNT. Those who ponder on casualties from the use of H-bombs reckon them not as individual deaths, but think of them by the millions, and the term megadeath has been introduced for the death of a million people. Within the six or eight-mile diameter circle of heavy blast and firestorm from a one-megaton bomb, more than a million people might die. This would mean something like a megadeath for a megaton. For smaller bombs the figure might run proportionately higher (at Hiroshima it was about 70 kilodeaths for 20 kilotons), and the figure of ten megatons would cause less than ten megadeaths, partly because the central part of a big city is not large enough and some of the less densely populated suburbs are included in the fourteen to eighteen-mile circle.

We may speak glibly of megadeaths, but to appreciate what a megadeath means, in human terms, we have to think in as personal a way as possible about the suffering and devastation, the loss of elements of civilization and of precious personal expectations within those dread circles. Perhaps it would be best to go back and read John Hersey's *New Yorker* account of the terrible, but in modern terms diminutive, tragedy of Hiroshima as seen in a dazed way by people on its periphery.[1]

Perhaps we should think of the suffering of a single person, like Joan of Arc, burned at the stake. Then we should think of hundreds of thousands of people being burned to death, some trapped under fallen timbers, some immobilized by broken bones, some simply surrounded by flames with no place better to go. Perhaps we should think of hundreds of thousands crouched in the corners of suburban basements, knowing of loved ones downtown who would never return, wondering about other loved ones perhaps crouched in other cellars but out of reach because of the radiation from fallout, wondering whether the radiation is mounting up to a harmful dose, living without electricty or heat or sanitary facilities and rationing the water from the water-heater tank to drink, wondering if there will be food when it will be safe to go out weeks later. Perhaps we should think of the injured—casualties from flying glass or skin burns, with skin peeling off and no one to bring help. If we are callous enough to dismiss all of this with the thought that it is the lot of humanity to suffer, then we may perhaps consider the greatest loss of all to be the loss of the facilities and the organization for higher thought and joyous living, the termination of institutions of culture and civilized cooperation which have been centuries a-building and which can probably never be resurrected if the bomb we have been speaking of is one of many bombs in a general war.

A WAR OF MANY H-BOMBS

So far we have been considering the damage caused by a single H-bomb of modest one-megaton size. This is a sort of unit, a small unit, in terms of which the calamity of nuclear war may be measured. (Perhaps we'll need a larger unit for convenience, and speak of a so-many kilobomb war.) It would be arrogant to claim to know what a nuclear war would be like, or what the world would be like thereafter. It goes much too far beyond our experience to permit of more than a guess. There is no question but that it would be terrible beyond previous human experience, but one may still question how terrible. One of the most serious unknowns is how many H-bombs would be used, and in particular how many would be used on cities.

In 1959, a congressional subcommittee held hearings on the effects of nuclear war, and spent a week taking testimony on what would happen if 263 H-bombs (averaging 5½ megatons apiece) hit specified targets in the United States. The slightly reassuring conclusion was reached that almost three quarters of the population would survive, and this was publicized in such a way as to almost give the impression that 263 is the authentic number of H-bombs that will hit the U.S. if there is a nuclear war. Of course, no such number can be given with confidence, especially if we don't know specifically whether we're talking about this year or ten or twenty years from now.

In contemplating whether it is desirable to keep the capability of nuclear war as a permanent arm of our foreign policy, desirable on the grounds of practical politics or on the grounds of morality (to be discussed in other chapters of the book) or on both grounds indistinguishably, we must be interested in the consequences of future nuclear weapons capabilities as well as in those of the present. If, in some judgment of political realism, nuclear weapons are now desirable or acceptable for ourselves and our potential adversaries but will be unacceptable because of the grim prospect of future weapons capabilities ten or twenty years from now, then it is high time for us to start now to supplement them with better arrangements for keeping peace at that later time.

Present stockpiles of the fission and fusion materials are adequate to make enough nuclear weapons to obliterate the major nations of the earth. Those 263 involved 1,446 megatons of explosive power, which is only about one-tenth of the unofficially estimated U.S. stockpile. The stockpile is, of course, growing, as is that of the Soviet Union, and they will be very much bigger ten years from now unless their growth is stopped by some agreement. That hypothetical attack, with roughly one-tenth of the present stockpile, was estimated to kill more than one-fourth of the U.S. population, thus leaving less than three-fourths to pick up the pieces and carry on as a perhaps recognizable but badly dismembered nation. The estimate was fifty million dead and twenty million seriously injured. After a bit of recovery, the nation would presumably be ready either for another round or for peace-keeping agreements that should have been made before the disaster. If in a war of about this magnitude the enemy had suffered even worse, it is possible that the agreement could be made on more favorable terms after than before the attack, but it is hardly conceivable that the difference in terms could be so great as to compensate for the disaster. As has been said by heads of state of both East and West, in a nuclear war both sides would lose.

We should not, however, examine the aftermath of a postulated war with a view to deciding whether our side might gain, as though we might be rationally planning to start such a war. The problem in assessing the consequences is to decide whether, in attempting to attain certain goals of policy without war, we are justified in *risking* the war. The purpose of such official investigations as the one we have referred to is ultimately to decide whether the war would be too disastrous to be worth risking for given objectives, and in this context the loss of a quarter of the population is seen by some as less than a complete disaster.

Some such number as 263 may be a reasonable estimate of the number of bombs that might fall in the first day or two of a nuclear war right now or two years ago, or perhaps two years hence. Even now, one might ask why an enemy determined enough to strike at all would deliver only about one-tenth of a stockpile. The real problem is one not so much of the size of the stockpile of nuclear warheads, but of the means of delivery. It may be that the primary vehicles now available can deliver no more, but that, after they have rather thoroughly crippled defenses against manned aircraft, these could be used as a secondary means of delivery to renew the attack.

With those who promote the view that we could now survive as a nation and can thus afford to use the threat of war as an instrument of foreign policy, the estimate of our ability to recover appears to be based on the very dubious assumption that, after a devastating blow destroying most of our cities and their populations, people would be properly motivated to go about the business of re-establishing an orderly community in an effective and efficient way. In fact, it is very hard to imagine what would happen. We have no experience with disaster on such a scale, far exceeding the capabilities of any rescue service that might survive. Imagine a truck driver, for example. His services are needed to transport food from areas where uncontaminated food might still be available to dispossessed people in other parts of the country. Normally he took instructions from his firm's headquarters in a city now destroyed, and received his weekly pay check according to a filing system that is no more, and went home to a family that could buy groceries with the pay check. Now there's none of that incentive left. His family is partly maimed, partly dead. He doesn't know if there will be food to buy if he does work. Probably hungry bands are roaming around, or he fears they are, raiding available food supplies, perhaps murdering as they plunder, and there is no prospect that the supplies will last long. Is he not more apt to join the raiders and try to stay with the remnants of his family than to go away to work? Is martial law with martial economic initiative the answer? Can it organize everybody's activity quickly and effectively amidst disaster conditions? Is there apt to be a subsequent return to personal freedom and a nation recognizable by its ideals? This scenario is presented not to suggest that any one guess about the postwar scene is valid, but merely to point out that there are grave questions

which have not been adequately answered about the real meaning of
a 263-bomb war producing fifty megadeaths, as a sample, in our
country.

So much for a war around 1962. Its numbers of bombs are limited
to some extent by the fact that the number of intercontinental ballistic
missiles on either side is considerably less than two or three hundred,
and the number of manned bombers getting through defenses, at
least in the first wave, might be limited to some such number by the
fact that they are approaching obsolescence.

But for the war of the future, it is not reasonable to postulate any
such small numbers. No effective defense against intercontinental
ballistic missiles is expected. Such missiles are a novelty now, but
military hardware has a way of multiplying indefinitely until it is
superseded by something more effective. With normal tendencies for
military expansion the number of hydrogen warheads quickly de-
liverable by long-range missiles will number in the thousands after a
decade or so. This vaguely suggests the dimensions of the war we should
be thinking about when we consider the practicability of nuclear war
and what efforts and sacrifices we should be willing to make to try to
avoid it.

We are loath to believe the realities of the growing threat of nuclear
war. Some people have derived solace from the estimate that nuclear
war, if it should come now, would still leave perhaps over half of
the population alive and unmaimed. After having been told that
nuclear war would mean annihilation, the prediction of anything
less comes as a relief. It fosters the optimistic belief that things will not
be so bad as the scientists and others say, after all. When the scientists
started crying havoc in the first years of the nuclear age, they spoke
of weapons to be developed fairly soon which would make nuclear
war a war of annihilation. Now we have seen how fast their prediction
is coming true. We have come far enough to reach war of quarter-
annihilation, so to speak, as a present threat. It should be no relief to
find ourselves so far on the way. We may be much farther than that.
And we cannot expect any new technical miracle to bail us out this
time. There will be technical advances, but almost surely none to
supersede the power of the hydrogen weapon or to provide an adequate defense against it. Political advances will be required for that.

If about 250 bombs would kill a quarter of the population, one might at first conclude that a thousand bombs, four times as many, would annihilate the whole population, but it is not quite so simple as that. Many of he choicest targest have already been included in the first 250, though not all of the dense city populations were so included in the congressional study we have mentioned. The additional weapons would yield diminishing returns, a larger proportion of them being partially wasted on smaller cities and suburban or rural areas. Many would be used against isolated missiles sites. Thus, an attack on the U.S. of a thousand H-weapons might spare a tenth or a quarter or perhaps even a third of the population from direct death by blast or fire.

But the chance of ultimately escaping the damaging effects of fallout becomes increasingly slim as the number of weapons gets this large or even larger. Here the effects of the many bombs are cumulative. What might have been a tolerable dose of radiation with 250 bombs can become fatal with the effects of a thousand all added up.

Until people in the U.S. suddenly became excited about shelters in 1961, fallout was discussed mainly in the context of peace-time nuclear weapons tests. Previously (mostly in 1952-54 and 1957-58) about two hundred atomic and hydrogen bomb tests were carried out (150 by the U.S. and Britain, about 50 by the U.S.S.R.). Many of these were A-bombs, and only something like a dozen were large H-bombs which contributed most of the worldwide fallout. There have been long debates and much disagreement among scientists and others as to whether or not the worldwide fallout from these few bombs was and is very harmful. That it is somewhat harmful there is no doubt, but the question concerns whether it is significantly harmful compared with all the other hazards and tragedies which beset the human race, and whether the harm is justified by the purposes of the tests.

In these tests, the bomb damage which is most awesome in war, that is, the direct effect of blast and fire, and even the "local" fallout extending several hundred or a thousand miles downwind, has been rendered harmless, or almost so, by careful choice of remote sites. The concern has been with the worldwide fallout which comes from the part of the bomb debris carried up high into the stratosphere by the heat of a big H-bomb. Once so high, much of it circulates around the world for months or years before falling down to earth in rain or snow. The elements strontium 90 and cesium 137 are the most serious culprits because they have a strong radiation and keep it for a long time, for about thirty years before it decays to half strength. They are culprits also because entering through food and milk they tend to find their way to the bone structure and thus to stay concentrated in parts of the human body, particularly the bodies of growing children, for a long time. A possible effect of such concentrations of radioactivity is cancer. How frequently it might occur is very uncertain, partly because the experimental evidence is mostly from mice, and it is men we are interested in.

Genetic misfortunes are another effect of radiation. They are the result partly of radiation from outside the body, such as from fallout particles settled on the ground, and partly of radioactive carbon which becomes part of the body. This type of damage might be a long time in showing up. Damage to a genetic cell may cause an abnormal birth in the first generation or the tenth. Once produced by H-bombs, radioactive carbon lasts thousands of years.

Among men who should know as much about these things as anyone, there is disagreement and doubt as to how serious are these effects from the few big bombs already tested. Scientists who know most about genetics seem to be among those most concerned. Attempts have been made to set limits of strontium 90 intake which are quite safe, say ten times below the level at which trouble might begin. Even before the 1961 Soviet tests the combined effects of a few U.S. bombs and a few Soviet bombs had begun to push those limits in the middle of the U.S. Wheat has been found a bit too radioactive in Minnesota after a Soviet test in Siberia. If we are anywhere near the safe limit in some parts of the world after just a few bombs, it seems quite certain that very dangerous levels will be reached in most of the world from world-wide fallout in a war of two thousand bombs—a thousand on the U.S. and a thousand on the U.S.S.R., for example. A war a decade from now may involve many more big bombs than that.

In the long run, the genetic damage appears particularly serious because of the way it accumulates from generation to generation. If a quarter of the population should emerge from the blast and escape lethal radiation sickness from the local fallout, it would still have to find ways of feeding itself from the land with its lingering radioactivity and to endure abnormal radiations for years. Despite abnormal incidence of cancer and many abnormal births, it would propagate itself. There would be either barbarism or civilization. If the latter, this would presumably continue to include nuclear-biological war as its most unpleasant characteristic. If one war with perhaps two thousand bombs had not already made genetic abnormalities so frequent as to distort or destroy the human race, a succession of wars with more bombs in later generations probably would. This is one possible outcome if either the first nuclear war or the second were not put off so long as to involve enough weapons to destroy the race completely.

There have been several literary treatments of nuclear disaster for the race, of which Neville Shute's *On the Beach* is perhaps the most impressive. Many who have read it or seen the motion picture have been deeply impressed with the threat of a nuclear end of the inhabited world, and have then been let down into a mood of incredulity and complacency by the report that the plot is technically incorrect. The plot was based on the use of cobalt bombs (bombs loaded with a special material to increase the radioactivity of a hydrogen bomb many times) in the northern hemisphere contaminating the atmosphere to a level lethal through radiation sickness, and on having the contamination gradually creep southward, mile by mile, across the southern hemisphere. This is inaccurate both because cobalt bombs will probably not be used, at least not in a first nuclear war, and also because the worldwide circulation of winds does not work that way. The novelist has taken some liberties in order to write a novel about the nuclear end of the world. A more realistic portrayal would be too horrible for his art. For men and women and children screaming in the flames he has substituted a gentle euthanasia inducing people to lie down and die mildly, on an inexorable schedule. That a novelist has overplayed the completeness and underplayed the horror of the act should be no grounds for ignoring the impact of his message.

SECONDARY ASPECTS OF NUCLEAR WARFARE

The overriding fact is that, unless the development of ever more insidious arsenals is arrested, nuclear warfare threatens such destruction as to mean an unimaginably horrible tragedy if it comes soon and the end of the human race if it comes later. Compared to this, other important considerations seem secondary, and they are too involved to receive more than inadequate mention in this brief discussion of a large subject.

The question of construction of fallout shelters as a part of "civil defense" has received some study and deserves more. It should be studied not only from the point of view of the number of people saved from immediate fallout if war does come—saved to emerge after a few weeks and face the problem of survival in spite of the contamination of food and water supplies and in spite of the terrific disorganization. It should be studied also from the point of view of its influence on the likelihood of war. One can argue this question both ways. Construction of shelters, along with underground construction of power supplies, vital factories, and storage of food and supplies, makes our country a less vulnerable target and thus less inviting to a potential aggressor. It may at least force him to prepare more weapons than he otherwise would. On the other hand, construction of shelters by one side, or sudden evacuation of city populations to rural shelters, might make it seem to the other side that the first strike was being prepared and invite a preemptive blow. In considering a national shelter program, it must be realized that there is little hope of constructing effective shelters for the survival of city populations, so these populations would probably be "written off" in a practicable program and attention concentrated on shielding rural populations, outside the range of fire and blast, against the most dangerous effects of local fallout in the first two or three weeks after an attack, in the hope that the attack would not soon be repeated.

Any temporary advantage in bargaining power that might be gained by one side through the building of shelters will probably be cancelled in the long run by a compensating shelter program on the other side. The decision concerning a really big civil defense program on both sides should not be made without considering it an important part of the decision whether to try by mutual understanding to modify the course of the arms race either by disarmament agreement or by the "more moderate and gradual changes" advocated in the preceding chapter. Such proposals will appeal more strongly to both sides if, in addition to reducing the likelihood of nuclear war, they avoid the very considerable unpleasantness of all-out civil defense preparations.

Another aspect of the nuclear age is the possibility of using "tactical" nuclear weapons in area warfare against enemy troop and supply concentrations near some semblance of a fighting front. This is apparently envisaged as something like the battlefield fighting of previous wars, with greatly increased firepower. The enveloping tactics of World

War II were so easily victorious early in the war because they faced a defense designed for the direct assault of World War I. It is not clear to what extent the present build-up of tactical arms is again getting us ready to fight the last war. Hopefully we will never learn the answer, for it would have to be by experience. In the past there has been time, after discovery of this mistake, to correct it and adapt to new conditions before the end of the war. In nuclear war the time scale will probably be much too short for that.

The reasoning behind the present preparation for large-scale "strategic" nuclear warfare is that the very grim prospect of nuclear war against a nation prepared to retaliate will deter any rational leader from attacking. Such preparation is known as a posture of deterrence. Its presumed effectiveness depends on its credibility. It is credible that the U.S.S.R. would react to the arrival of several U.S. missiles on Soviet cities with an all-out nuclear thrust, or vice versa. Thus each side is deterred from direct attack on the homeland of the other, if we assume there might be reason to want to attack. It is much less credible that the U.S. would react in the same way to a Soviet attack on, let us say, Pakistan, for such reaction would probably mean quarter-annihilation or more of the U.S., in retaliation. Thus the great strategic deterrent may be ineffective to deter relatively small aggressions. The rationale of tactical nuclear weapons is the hope that they may be effective in such cases. Credibility here depends on the leaders' believing, whether it is true or not, that tactical nuclear weapons could be used in local situations without triggering a large-scale nuclear war. Between the great nuclear powers, this proposition is extremely dubious. It might be true in a hypothetical war between, for example, China and Indonesia if these should both acquire tactical nuclear weapons and none larger, for in this case one of the great nuclear powers might not feel obliged to come to the rescue. But in such a field of conflicting vital interests as Europe, or between the great nuclear powers directly, it seems quite unlikely that the passions of war would permit stopping at some definite number of kilotons of nuclear weapon power. Eventually, the losing side would be too much tempted to unleash more and more powerful weapons. "Tactical" nuclear weapons are in general smaller than most "strategic" weapons. They include the "small" twenty-kiloton size, like the two bombs formerly used strategically to destroy two Japanese cities, and also much smaller ones right down to the power of conventional chemical bombs.

There is no distinct dividing line between a small nuclear weapon and a large one. There is a distinct dividing line between conventional and nuclear weapons. No matter how "small," nuclear weapons are definitely recognizable by their radioactive products. For this reason, tactical nuclear weapons, although they provide relatively cheap fire-power, cannot be considered as an adequate substitute for conventional forces as a deterrent to small-scale war. Any war might escalate into the big nuclear war that nobody wants. All war is therefore so dangerous as to be obsolete in the nuclear age, from a rational point of view, even though it may seem inevitable. But a tactical nuclear war between full-fledged nuclear powers or their closest allies is particularly apt to trigger the great calamity.

SOURCES OF NUCLEAR WAR

World politics is dominated by "two atomic colossi eyeing each other (more or less) malevolently across a divided world," to adopt President Eisenhower's phrase. There are many world issues in which they have important stakes and on which they disagree, but particularly is this the case with how the countries emerging from colonial rule are to be encouraged in the development of their own capabilities and of economic and cultural ties with the contending big nations. Until rules can be agreed upon effectively governing the nature of this contest without recourse to the threat of force, we cannot expect to get rid of the precarious system of deterrence as the basis of peace. Development toward the acceptability of such a step should be the primary goal of constructive statesmanship, but it may take a long time.

There is very serious danger of nuclear war breaking out before such a goal can be reached. Among the possible causes of the war that nobody wants, are war by accident, by misjudgment, by escalation, or by catalysis. When the warning time is only a few minutes and the system is designed to get missiles on their way before the enemy's missiles have hit, technical accident is all too possible. Great precautions are of course taken, but they must work infallibly, year after year, in hundreds of installations all over the globe. A radar picket could have prevented the calamity of Pearl Harbor, but it failed through error in human judgment on the one critical day. It is of interest to know that some Soviet scientists are just as deeply concerned from personal conviction about the danger of accidental war as are some in the West.

War by escalation means the growth of a small war into a big one. A border incident might start a small conventional war in which tactical nuclear weapons might be used by both sides, whereupon the more hard-pressed side might use larger and larger nuclear weapons.

War by miscalculation refers particularly to the system of threat and counter threat, or bluff and counter bluff, by which nations seek to settle differences with the expectation of not actually going to war. It is a delicate operation, and there is too much danger that a genuine threat may be misjudged as a bluff, or a point may be reached where lack of response would mean complete loss of credibility.

Catalysis means the setting off of a big reaction by a small agent which may itself escape harm. With the many nuclear nations of the future, madmen as heads of state are not impossible. If two small nuclear nations are about to go to war, a national leader might, for example, think he could avoid it by starting a war between two big nations. With nuclear missiles popping up out of the sea from submarines, it will be virtually impossible to ascertain the source of an attack.

The situation will grow more dangerous, in the long run, if no political steps are taken to alter a normal sequence of military developments. The continued refinement of weapons will make sudden surprise attack increasingly effective, and lead to a more trigger-sensitive situation. The proliferation of weapons, both in number within the present nuclear nations and in the number of nuclear nations, will increase the possible sources of war. The anticipation of the many-nuclear-nation problem, or "n'th-nation problem," is particularly pressing at this time. Unless we change our course, there will probably be a dozen nuclear nations within a decade or two.

DIPLOMATIC DEVICES TO AVOID NUCLEAR WAR

The undoing of the human race may be that its technical advances have been so rapid that its statecraft can never catch up. Against nuclear attack no technical defense is expected to be adequate. The only adequate defense must be political. In thinking of the practicality—or of the morality—of nuclear war preparations, we must do so against the background of the possible political alternatives, and the sacrifices that may be necessary to achieve them.

A nuclear test-ban agreement[2] is proposed because it would slow down the development of the arms race to a significant degree without demanding that the great nuclear nations abandon the posture of deterrence on which they now rely for keeping the peace. It might be acceptable both because it appeals to the mutual interest of East and West in reducing the likelihood of war and because it makes minimum demands on changing of national attitudes. It also eliminates the difficulties of fallout from tests. Since no progress toward worldwide agreement is possible until the great nuclear powers agree on the details of controls to be introduced, the purpose of the Geneva negotiations has been to arrive at such a great-power agreement in the hope that statesmanship would then persuade the other significant nations to adhere to it. It would be in the self-interest of each non-nuclear nation to adhere to it, in order to make possible this degree of restraint by the nuclear powers and by other non-nuclear nations.

A test ban will clearly not end the arms race. It is not so much a measure of arms control as arms-development control. It will prevent the development of ever more insidious weapons by the nuclear nations, but will not prevent further stockpiling of the warheads they now know how to make. It would be particularly effective in controlling weapons development if it could be coupled with a missile-test ban, which was not included in the negotiations. A nuclear test ban would prevent the development of an atomic arsenal by other nations. Thus, if nuclear nations refrain from transferring nuclear weapons to others, a test ban would be an effective answer to the n'th-nation problem.

The negotiations during 1958-61 dragged on longer than seemed necessary for several reasons. Probably most important was a lack of advance preparation on both sides. The Soviets apparently wanted a controlled test ban agreement, or at least so it seemed until in 1961 they introduced a demand for tripartite administration of the control organization, but they were dickering to get as little interference as possible with their military secrecy. Secrecy about the exact location of missile launching sites is a legitimate element of military strength in which they enjoy an advantage. The attempt is being made to design a test-ban control system so that inspectors sent out to investigate an earthquake and make sure it is not an underground test will not have much chance of finding a missile site. The Soviets were seeking to keep this likelihood extremely— even unreasonably—small. Another reason for the drawn-out negotiations is that the U. S. administration, at least up until 1961, vascillated because it never made a clear and united decision on how seriously it wanted a test ban and which set of advisors to heed. This was one aspect of inadequate preparation. It points strongly to the need for a greatly expanded National Peace Agency or Disarmament Administration to explore such matters in advance.

The technical questions associated with the test ban are too involved to receive adequate discussion here. Almost all tests in the past have been in the atmosphere where testing is easiest and most effective. These can be observed from afar. The negotiations have contemplated a network of seismic stations to guard against the possibility of underground tests.

The fear has been expressed by some that a few comparatively small tests carried out underground evading a test-ban agreement might permit the USSR to make advances to place them ahead of us, but such fears seem greatly exaggerated. The clandestine tests would have to be carried out under very difficult and restricted conditions, and could not be used to test the big H-bombs which constitute the most important part of the nuclear arsenal. It is technically possible to construct an enormous cavity deep underground, much larger than any ever made, and to hide a test in it of a bomb perhaps as big as one percent of the power of a big H-bomb. The seismic signals could thus be kept too weak to be identified by the initial detection system discussed at Geneva. The problem of doing this without having the construction job observed is so formidable, and the incentives for doing so are so small, that the chance of its actually happening seems almost nil. Such fears have been based partly on misconceptions concerning the possibilities of developing a neutron bomb and a fission-free-fusion bomb.

The neutron bomb, which has been the subject of definite planning and probably really could be developed with further testing, is a small and specialized weapon, not different from an A-bomb in fundamental principle, but pared down in such a way that its blast is less damaging than its neutron radiation. It causes radioactive contamination in proportion to its power, and thus less than the more powerful normal A-bomb. Its neutrons go out in all directions and kill people nearby quickly. Beyond this short distance, and out to some greater distance of perhaps a few hundred yards, the neutrons will give people radiation sickness and condemn them to die within a few days. This has dubious military effectiveness, for the doomed soldiers can act as desperate fighters for a few hours or days. There are other disadvantages of the prospective neutron bomb, such as its high cost in terms of fissionable material and the likelihood that it will trigger the use of larger nuclear weapons.

The fission-free-fusion bomb, on the other hand, is at the stage of being a scientist's pipe dream. It will probably never be developed, or at least not until technology has progressed to a much more advanced stage many years from now, but if it were possible, it could be a big bomb and, for its size, a quite "clean" bomb. ("Clean" means less prolific of radioactive contamination than a normal A-bomb.) It would be cheap in terms of the special materials used, so that it could be made in quantity by small countries as well as large ones. It would destroy mainly by blast and heat, as does the H-bomb. There is some hopeful talk about using fission-free-fusion bombs as anti-missile missiles, their relative cleanliness being an advantage over friendly territory. Yet, not only the memory of Pearl Harbor, but also the intrinsic nature of the problem should convince us that it is illusory to expect the nuclear-age problem to be solved by an effective defense against nuclear ballistic missiles. A partially effective defense would merely escalate attack requirements. Even if the fission-free-fusion bomb should become suddenly available to one or both of the big powers, it wouldn't seriously upset the balance because the main holdup is in delivery vehicles, not in quantity of H-bombs. Although it almost surely can't be made, it would be ironic if the two great nuclear powers, through the intensity of their rivalry and with their superior developmental resources, should develop this weapon only to have the information become available to many nations and put them both in greater danger.

For the moment the Soviets show no desire at all for a controlled test ban unless coupled with complete disarmament. If they persist, we have through excessive caution and exaggerated fears lost a fleeting opportunity to try to modify the arms race by this means. This should warn us not to procrastinate on bold but controlled steps to disarmament. But perhaps policy may yet again swing toward a test ban, for this still seems to hold advantages for both sides.

In the fall of 1961, two of the new developments were, first, the sudden resumption of large-scale testing of nuclear weapons in the atmosphere by the Soviets, ending a three-year moratorium and, second, the establishment by Congress of the U.S. Arms Control and Disarmament Agency for the more intensive study of possible alternatives to the unlimited arms race. The test resumption seems to indicate that the Soviets changed their minds about wanting a test ban some time before the sudden unreasonableness of their "Troika" demand for a three-man test-ban administration in early 1961, and that they were probably negotiating in Geneva with tongue in cheek at least since then. Their tests were mainly of quite large nuclear weapons. This seems to corroborate the view of those in our country who favored a test ban in 1958 on the grounds that a very few small underground clandestine tests, even if they could be carried out under a fairly well-controlled test ban, would be of small military value compared with the big tests which would be stopped by the ban. Those who then opposed a test ban (unless it could have completely "foolproof" controls) and who effected our withdrawal from our negotiating position late in 1958, did so out of seemingly exaggerated fears of the possible military consequences of small clandestine tests. Now that the Soviets have gone ahead and reaped the military advantage of the big tests, as they could not have done under a test ban, our reluctance to negotiate at that time seems to have meant one more lost opportunity to try to modify the arms race when it would have been advantageous to do so. The Geneva negotiations recessed after the recent test resumption, but a test ban remains almost as desirable as ever, even though the Soviets have probably learned more from their new test series than we from ours (because they presumably had more to learn). Whether Soviet (and Chinese) policy will ever (again) swing towards a test ban, or whether we may have to include a test ban in a larger arms-control package to interest them, remains to be seen. The studies of the new Arms Control and Disarmament Agency should facilitate our finding out, particularly if it is ever adequately staffed and funded to become a large operation.

A test-ban agreement introduced now would make further steps in arms control easier at a later date. By preventing the arms of the future from becoming still more refined, it would reduce the danger from weapons which might possibly be hidden in evasion of a future arms-control agreement. But its main contribution would be in exploring the way toward mutual confidence in control measures and in nurturing a climate of opinion more favorable to further agreement. A test ban has very real value in itself. It may be reasonably adopted with a firm resolve that it does not necessarily imply any further disarmament steps, and that further steps must be taken only on their own merits at the time. An opponent of disarmament may appreciate the value of a test ban and favor it as a separate item. A proponent of disarmament is apt also to favor a workable test ban partly because it would give us new information about how control systems work which should later make disarmament seem still more attractive.

The terms "disarmament" and "arms control" are sometimes used interchangeably, for far-reaching disarmament surely does control arms. On the other hand, measures of arms control are being advocated which are not disarmament. One proposal is simply to put our missiles in well-protected sites and to encourage the Soviet Union to do the same. This sort of action by mutual understanding without formal agreement would in a sense control arms, but not disarm. Such arms control is merely self-control. The reasoning behind it is that it is in the self-interest of each to convince the other that it is not planning to strike, for then the one need not be so trigger-sensitive as to jeopardize the other. Missiles on open launching pads, the way some are now being installed in western U. S., foolishly near cities, are provocative of war. They could not survive an attack, and thus have no "second strike capability." They appear to the other side to be useful only for one thing, for a surprise attack. Since we don't intend to launch a surprise attack, they probably do us more harm than good. Their principal military justification is that they increase the Soviet first-strike requirement, but they are grouped ineffectively for that.

Another proposal for arms-self-control is to depend for deterrence entirely on Polaris missiles in submarines and to encourage the Soviets to do the same. The advantage of this is that these weapons are presumably so invulnerable that there would be no need for very quick decisions in the event of a limited attack. Thus response times could be longer, allowing time to learn whether the attack might have come by accident. If all nuclear nations would somehow refrain from making cheaper installations, another advantage might be that the high cost of the submarines would keep the numbers down, so that wars might be less than kilobomb wars. But such a scheme would not solve the n'th-nation problem. Some propose that it should be coupled with a "pax Russo-Americana" to do that. Instead, it might combine well with a test ban.

Thus there is a type of arms-control scheme which proposes to modify but not end the arms race, keeping such a high level of arms in one category that small infringements in others may be tolerated and no detailed inspection considered necessary; on this perhaps no formal agreement is required. Such proposals demand little and buy little. They do buy something—a considerable reduction in the likelihood of accidental war—and that is distinctly better than nothing if no more may be had.

There is much to be said for trying to go much further with disarmament soon, paying more in the way of departure from our conventional ways of thinking but buying much more long-range safety to make it worth while. In fact, it might well turn out that this is the only approach on which we could get sufficient Soviet cooperation and agreement, so we may be faced with a choice between this and the completely uncontrolled arms race with its probably calamitous consequences. Such an approach seems appropriate because it has a novelty commensurate with the technical challenge of the nuclear age.

Past disarmament negotiations have encountered the difficulty, among others, that military secrets and free access of inspectors, like oil and water, don't mix. If two distrustful men have guns pointing at each other but want to let them down, each wants to be sure he doesn't let his down first. Disarmament should proceed by gradual stages so neither side lets down its guard all at once. This means that some military force and important military secrets are retained while inspectors verify compliance with the first stages of disarmament during which it may be feared that the inspectors will discover those secrets. To avoid this, the best plan now available is the "region-by-region disarmament plan" proposed recently by several people, in part by Dr. M.

Mooney in New York and Professor A. P. Alexandrov in Moscow, but in its most refined form by Professor Sohn of Harvard.[3] In this plan, each country to be disarmed divides itself into six regions of equal military value and submits to an international control authority a report on how many military installations of various kinds it has in each region. The regions are to be disarmed one after another at one-year intervals, but no one knows in advance which one will come first. At a certain time the region to be disarmed first in each country is suddenly chosen by the authority and inspectors are quickly sent to close off arms transport from such regions. Lists are then submitted giving the exact location of the military installations already reported in these regions so the inspectors can disarm them. There are no longer any geographical military secrets, like missile sites, in these first-chosen regions and the inspectors are then free to hunt throughout them for possible violations. This provides a check on the original report on a random-sample basis, thus establishing confidence in the report for all regions. The gradual growth of confidence is very helpful as one proceeds to the other regions in the same way, especially as the last region is approached. It will probably take longer than six years to develop an acceptable decision-and-command organization for an international police force, to eliminate the need for deterrence by the individual nations. If it does, then some arrangement must be made to discourage attack during an interim period. Thus it may be agreed in advance that, when it is time to disarm the last region in each country, some inspected and controlled military force is to be retained in each of the great nuclear powers, as a "transitional deterrent." For example, the U.S. and the U.S.S.R. might each retain fifty missiles distributed in a secret way between two hundred well-protected sites, with the privilege of shifting them periodically within certain regional groups of sites. The inspectors may then be permitted to see only one group of sites at a time, so neither side ever knows where more than a few of the other's missiles are, yet they are all reliably counted. This would provide a reliable deterrent for the interim period with much less danger of accidental war than is inherent in the present proliferating arms race.

Fifty modern missiles would be enough to inflict on either country losses which would be inacceptable to any rational leader. What we or the Soviets do in Berlin, for example, does not depend on how big the deterrent is beyond fifty missiles, but on the existence of a reliable deterrent threatening inacceptable losses if invoked. This disarmament proposal does not require solution of the world's problems before being put into effect. It provides instead a safer way to wait for and work for solution of the world's problems.

Many will consider it unduly idealistic or naive. It is far more naive to believe, as most people do, that we can go on for decades with our present arms race without experiencing nuclear calamity. What stands in the way of our having the serious national goal to do all we can to negotiate such a far-reaching disarmament agreement? With the region-by-region plan available, it is no longer so much the technical difficulty of the problem that stands in the way, though that is considerable. It is more the tendency of most people to take the conservative view, to think they learn all from past experience, to suspect new thought about the new situation, and to believe that the best defense is to be psychologically ready to do something rather like fighting the last war. In later chapters, other authors discuss the moral aspects of nuclear war. The moral question comes closest to home for each of us in asking ourselves whether we are moral in permitting, partly through our own complacency, the preservation among us of attitudes which forbid our making a rational decision on disarmament as a vital national goal.

Recognizing that real difficulties would have to be solved in a radical and unprecedented manner to make disarmament possible, some thinkers claim that this goal is therefore Utopian. Those who consider that a careful and determined quest for disarmament is instead a practical objective include some physical scientists who remember a time when the A-bomb was only an impracticable dream. There were a few general principles to suggest that it could perhaps be made if what then seemed like superhuman efforts could sweep away terrific technical and fiscal obstacles. The determined team-work of a large organization of dedicated individuals of very different skills did overcome the difficulties quite quickly, and in retrospect it doesn't even sound difficult. While international human problems are very different from technical problems, it seems frustrating that no such extensive and determined effort has ever been devoted to the problems of arms controls and disarmament. (A beginning has been made by several small groups.) The new Arms Control and Disarmament Agency needs the political and psychological support of all thoughtful people if it is to develop into such an effort. We must eliminate from our national thinking the kind of complacency which, by too quickly using the label "Utopian," discourages turning this effort and all national policy towards a satisfactory long-term solution of the nuclear dilemma.

NOTES

1. John Hersey, *The New Yorker*, XXII (No. 29, 1946), p. 15.
2. D. R. Inglis, "Testing and Taming of Nuclear Weapons," New York, Public Affairs Pamphlets, No. 303 (1960); "Excessive Fear of Test-Ban Evasion," *Bulletin of the Atomic Scientists*, XVI, May, 1960, p. 168.
3. Louis B. Sohn, "Disarmament and Arms Control by Territories," *Bulletin of the Atomic Scientists*, XVII, April, 1961, p. 130. Earlier formulations were privately circulated in mimeographed form: "Disarmament through Territorial Demilitarization" by Louis B. Sohn in December, 1959, and "Total Disarmament by Territorial Divisions" by Melvin Mooney in February, 1960.

Ethical aspects
of the nuclear dilemma

BY KENNETH W. THOMPSON

Political and military problems throughout history have confronted statesmen with choices that impose greater moral burdens than many politicians, philosophers or reformers acknowledge or express. The successful politician can ill-afford to frame his approach in terms that suggest uncertainty about policy issues for his stock and trade lies in being affirmative and positive. Nor can (those) philosophers, conceiving their task as establishing systems of order and coherence within reality, linger too long over incoherences. The reformer if he sees painful conflicts between moral purposes or policies is impelled to contrive institutions or blue prints of Utopia that will simplify or rationalize the decisions future leaders will make. It has remained for historians like Thucydides or political theorists such as Aristotle or Plato, Hobbes or Locke to do justice to the perennial problems of political choice. Their function has been to ask whether and when "might makes right," if justice for the strong is the equivalent of justice for the weak, and under what circumstances the sanctions of law and order are accepted by men and states.

The problem of nuclear weapons is part and parcel of the international political power struggle today. The issues are incredibly complex; not even the wisest scientist or statesman can encompass them all. The citizen may be tempted to seek out a path of least resistance. He may denounce the whole terrifying process of building up deterrent force and call on his country unilaterally to renounce its defenses. Or alternatively, he may shut out from view events that are distasteful to moral consciousness and "leave the whole unhappy realm" to cynics, militarists and power politicians.

The historic conception of political ethics in western thought, at least in its more profound expressions, repudiates both these approaches. It must reject the nuclear pacifism that would leave America defenseless against Soviet tyranny for the same reason it rejected traditional pacifism as normative. It must also reject no less a posture of withdrawal from all the vital problems of politics, for this is a false alternative. A viable ethic must deal realistically with the problems of power and all the perennial issues they raise.

AMERICAN APPROACHES TO POWER

For more than a century America has proved itself singularly inept in coming to terms with the problems of power and force. Beginning as early as 1840, there were organized expressions of public feeling proclaiming deep-seated suspicion of diplomacy or force. The "peace movement" had as its goal the substitution for force of legal procedures like arbitration—which was the first expression of the peace movements to receive governmental sanction—and other forms of moral suasion.

Arbitration had served nations well at the turn of the century on issues which had not proved amenable to diplomacy. Settlements like the *Alabama* Claims case and the Bering Sea fisheries dispute were fresh in the public mind, and it was not surprising that the question should be asked why, if settlements like these had been possible, the same principles should not be applied to all our differences. It was forgotten that states reserve to themselves decisions on matters where vital interests are at stake. The United States itself had refused arbitration on the issue of the sinking of the *Maine,* which touched off the Spanish-American War, and no thoughtful person could have imagined the United States agreeing in advance to bind itself to arbitrate problems involving the Monroe Doctrine or our strategic interests in Panama or the Caribbean.

The problems of power have obviously been magnified by the sharp rise in the magnitude of force. Nearly four decades ago Prime Minister Herbert Asquith observed that science was beginning to "lisp the alphabet of annihilation." The dangers are daily borne in upon us not only of mutual devastation in war but also of radioactive poison in peace. Yet in the hydrogen era our approach to the problem of force has been curiously reminiscent of earlier days. The number of words and proposals devoted to a generalized attack on the disarmament problem perhaps exceeds attention to any comparable problem. Whereas before World War II the approach was one of erecting a system of fixed legal and arbitral procedures culminating in broad over-all legislation outlawing war—the Kellogg-Briand Pact—the postwar design has called for almost endless exchanges with Soviet delegates within the United Nations and outside, all looking toward the banning of the use of force, at least in certain of its forms, or to its control and regulation.

The dread disease which has tended to paralyze American thinking on the problem of force has its roots in at least three conditions of the American mind. We have assumed that force could be dealt with in the isolated compartments of disarmament conventions or arbitral treaties divorced from the harsh realities of power in the outside world or from viable strategic doctrines evolved to meet mutual interests and needs. We have favored a legal over a diplomatic approach. We have preferred to think in absolute rather than discriminate terms and to see force as a single-edged weapon that others might draw in a violent cause. In consequence, perhaps there is no area of international life where success has been more fleeting and where the best efforts of men supremely endowed have been greeted with more modest achievements.

Our prevailing approaches ignore the fact that the military establishments of nations still remain the most explicit element of foreign policy. Diplomacy and military strength appear to go hand in hand. In an earlier day, the great powers sent gunboats up the rivers of states they were seeking to influence. Today in the cold war the postwar distribution of power is closely related to the position of the Red Army at strategic points in the heart of Europe or to the latest technological development. Germany's demonically successful diplomacy in the interwar period must be seen as an outgrowth of superior military preparedness coupled with failure of the western Allies to organize their resources and power effectively. The explosion and testing of atom weapons by the Soviet Union or their launching of sputniks and lunik has consistently been followed by periodic and deliberate strategic moves in the cold war. Soviet behavior at various stages in the cold war has reflected Soviet confidence that their superior power made concessions and reasonable negotiations unnecessary.

Nevertheless, the difficulties inherent in maintaining military establishments that will not suffer defeat grow increasingly more complex. A nation may clearly recognize the need for military organs capable of supporting the foreign policies it pursues, but be limited in the margin of its economic resources that can be turned to military use. Some countries exhaust their resources in attaining a viable economy; others like the United States have a surplus with which to meet their foreign military and political commitments. A smaller power like Belgium may not be able to devote the same part of its gross national product to military ends as can the Soviet Union or the United States. Thus the problem of military establishments for the smaller powers, including the newer states, may in some instances take on a special character even though smaller dictatorships may escape this restriction for a given period.

But the problem of military security is equally perplexing for the great powers. If the present crisis between East and West were a simple clash either of military systems or political ideologies, we would doubtless face the future with more assurance and hope. However, because of the dual nature of the Soviet threat, we tend to vacillate between a military and ideological view of the struggle. The problem of arriving at valid and acceptable policies is at root the problem of defining the nature of the crisis. The uncertainty we feel about policies is basically an uncertainty over the crisis. There is irony in this perplexity because most informed observers in the early days of the cold war were convinced that the Russian threat to western civilization was identical with the Nazi menace. As such, men assumed the recipe for dealing with it was the same. It was said that if our leaders had learned anything from over two centuries of national experience, it was that foreign policy divorced from strength is impotent—a lesson not shared by all the people.

Seen from this approach, the immediate military threat can be interpreted as unquestionably the gravest danger. Those who hold to this view call for ever greater urgency in the multiplication of more powerful weapons of destruction, for new strategic doctrines, for hardened missile bases, and a nuclear weapons pool. The irreconcilable conflicts and tensions of the cold war will come to an end only when one side or the other forges decisively ahead. This trend of thought prompts a state to bestow the most lethal weapons on its allies and to continue indefinitely the multiplication of larger numbers of the most deadly instruments of war.

Some of our friends abroad have warned against too much preoccupation with armaments especially in light of their suicidal nature. However, the contradictory reactions in the newer states to thermonuclear devices is best seen in the effects of the sputniks. In the same countries that urge us to disarm, American prestige and virtue suffered a grievous blow when the Soviet Union launched the first satellite. Despite continuous criticism of America throughout Asia and Africa for its materialism and preoccupation with purely technological and military advance, confidence in American policy is gauged by the standards by which in another context our conduct has been deplored. We are reminded once more of Europe's and Asia's response when the U.S., through the United Nations, held the line in Korea. Then, our sharpest critics (including some in India who had found us rigidly anti-Communist and obsessed with the military threat) applauded the successful deployment of American power particularly until the fateful crossing of the 38th parallel.

Assuming then that the present crisis is partly but not exclusively military in nature, other problems must be faced. Three errors are commonly made in appraising the military component of foreign policy. First, military power is often confused with national power, and a nation's capacity to impose its will is equated with its military establishment. In reality, military power is like the fist whose force depends on the health and vitality of the body politic and the strength of the whole society. Troops in being are an important determinant of a successful foreign policy, but without other foundations they will not suffice. Second, the military element is often viewed in more static terms than is appropriate. The democracies in two world wars, while they have been the last to arm, have rallied their forces to gain victory in the end. Third, it is difficult to analyze and foresee the most effective distribution of the components of military force. For example, what comprises a strong military force today? Is it large ground forces, hydrogen bombs or intensive research? Is a small highly specialized army more desirable than a large number of ground forces, or are both essential for a nation that seeks to be strong?

The answer to these questions will probably be decisive in determining future influence in the world of states, yet it is sobering that estimates must be made on the basis of contingencies that cannot be foreseen. We know in a general way that an effective foreign policy must be supported by a military program that can safeguard national security. But this leaves those who make decisions with the painful task of distributing resources among alternative means of defense without any certainty of the kind of war they may have to fight.

Beyond this, the weapons of today may not be used in future wars because technology has rendered them obsolete. It is said that conventional weapons are fast being supplanted by new and more deadly weapons and therefore traditional armaments fail to provide an adequate basis for foreign policy. On the other hand, there are military experts who question whether atomic and hydrogen weapons will ever be used, given the prospect of mutual annihilation. Is it not fair then to ask whether the stockpiling of an unlimited supply of weapons that no nation would dare to use furnishes a state with the requisite military support? If so, a military establishment grounded in conventional weapons may fall short of providing an adequate defensive military posture, but so may a policy aimed at superior atomic capacities. This constitutes the crucial challenge in the armaments field with which both defense strategists and disarmament negotiators must cope today.

THE UNIQUENESS OF THE PRESENT ARMAMENTS PROBLEM

The United States has endeavored since World War II to build up western power so that the Soviet Union might not be tempted, as were the Nazis, to expand its empire through threats and aggression. In applying this principle which is theoretically sound, the West has confronted practical problems arising from the uniqueness of the present armaments problem. Military strength today requires both conventional and nuclear capacities but both economic considerations and the moral factor set restraints on arms programs.

Moral restraints may work to influence the course of an armaments race in two respects. They may generate the motive force for attempts at general disarmament or may prompt discriminate judgments on the limitation or channeling of armaments buildups. The literature of peace movements in the United States and Britain has concentrated primarily on the overall reduction and elimination of armaments. Such an approach is particularly congenial to the sensitive moral conscience. By and large, most proponents of general disarmament have favored a test ban with firm safeguards if possible but without if necessary. This school of thought has unquestionably induced western leaders to bend every effort to achieve disarmament. It has given a sense of urgency to disarmament programs and focussed the spotlight of public attention on the threat.

Yet the moral dignity of an alternative approach deserves mention. The ideas of restraint, proportionality and limitation have an important place in moral theory. Restraint in these terms might mean that nuclear weapons not be multiplied beyond the point where they serve a security function. The principle of proportionality assumes that the means employed are proportionate to the goal undertaken. For example, the United States seeks to deter the Soviet Union through its nuclear armaments program, but not to assure total military victory. This in itself sets limits to any armaments program, but moral considerations reinforce the limitation. A nation which says its objective is national and international security is obligated to pursue armaments programs that faithfully reflect this purpose. It can hardly engage in an unlimited buildup of weapons if these carry no clear implication for security purposes.

Restraint and proportionality may commend a renewed stress on conventional armaments as distinct from accelerating nuclear weapons programs. They may mean that hardening existing missile sites is more acceptable than adding to the missile stockpile. The development of mobile striking power may be politically more imperative and morally more defensible than unrestrained nuclear buildup. These various strategies may be both morally and politically preferable; earlier political theorists stressed the marriage of the ethical and the political in the virtue of prudence. Sometimes in politics restraint and prudence are the highest obtainable moral position. Political wisdom involves a weighing of moral and political considerations and a sound judgment, in Lincoln's phrase, "to do the best you can." It requires an estimate made in light of all the facts of what nations can do under existing circumstances.

Particularly the West, confronting a numerically superior rival, has been forced to turn its major efforts to the development of nuclear weapons. In so doing, its leaders face three crucial questions that weigh heavily on the minds of the citizenry: 1) What are the short and long-range hazards of nuclear weapons testing? 2) What are the prospects of a limited atomic war and its effects on the human race? and 3) What are the chances of survival in all-out nuclear conflict? If national security is based on some degree of nuclear capacity, responsible leaders must seek answers to these questions.

The hazards of nuclear weapons testing

Military and scientific advisors disagree at some point on all three questions but within the debate there are areas of agreement that can be identified. Public opinion at home and abroad is deeply troubled by the hazards of atomic tests. The perils of modern weapons lie not only in war but in weapons tests before the outbreak of conflict. For the first time in history, armaments imperil civilization even before warfare has broken out. Partly in response to this, both the United

States and Great Britain suspended nuclear tests on October 31, 1958. As far as could be determined the Soviet Union conducted no tests from November 3, 1958, through the summer of 1961. Some observers assert that underground tests are more difficult to detect than sometimes imagined and can be obscured by natural movements like earthquakes. They insist the Russians could have exploded nuclear devices that went undetected even in advance of the later round of tests.

Various panels and commissions have dealt with the problem of nuclear fall-out, one of the most recent being the Special Subcommittee on Radiation of the Joint Committee on Atomic Energy. Through public hearings held in May of 1959, the Subcommittee undertook to bring up to date the scientific information developed in 1957. It is on the basis of such inquiries that a highly provisional estimate can be made of the dangers of fall-out reflecting no clear-cut general conclusions but serving to sketch in the boundaries of the problem.

Some of the findings to date are reassuring in a limited sense. Until the fall of 1961, radiation from fall-out was but a small fraction of radiation from natural background sources in the earth and atmosphere. Men have of course had time to acclimate themselves to radiation from these sources while we are now confronted by a sudden disturbance brought about by humanly caused events. Nonetheless the citizen has a right to know that the excessive and unparalleled contamination some observers report appears not to correspond with the facts.

Authorities estimated that the amount of radio-active material blasted into the atmosphere and stratosphere by the nuclear powers resulted from a total of ninety to ninety-two megatons of fission explosions up to September, 1961. Nearly half this material was produced by Soviet and American tests in 1957 and 1958 before the last moratorium. If tests had not been resumed, the concentration of strontium 90 in human bones from past weapons tests would have reached a maximum in the period of 1962-1965. For the world's population, the average concentration then is estimated at seven strontium units.

This amount is relatively small compared to the natural background radiation levels or the maximum permissible concentration of sixty-seven units cited by such groups as the International Commission on Radiological Protection and the National Committee on Radiation Protection. If cycles of testing continued over the next two generations, however, in the pattern of tests of the five years preceding the moratorium, the predicted average concentration of strontium 90 would be forty-eight strontium units, a figure much more nearly approaching the danger point.

Scientific opinion is also divided on how fall-out material enters the food chain and the degree of damage fall-out can cause when it comes in contact with the human body. If there is no definitive answer to the central question of the amount of biological damage to present and future generations through increasing levels of fall-out, there are nonetheless important areas in which dangers and warning signs can be discerned. Experts call attention to a series of newly observed potential problems and hazards. They urge an increasing emphasis on the so-called "hot-spot" problem. They note that since 1957 the fall-out levels in certain areas may be unusually high. "Hot-spots" covering several square miles are created when rain washes radio-active material out of an air mass containing a fairly high concentration of radio-active particles as in a cloud from a recent test.

Beyond this, the distribution of world-wide fall-out is not uniform. About two-thirds of the stratospheric material is found in the Northern Hemisphere and about one-third in the Southern Hemisphere. The heaviest concentration is located in the Northern Hemisphere from 20 to 60 degrees north reflecting the fact that most of the tests have been conducted north of the equator. This also suggests that important areas in the United States fall within the zone of greatest exposure.

New problems also arise in connection with the so-called short-lived fission products such as strontium 89, barium 140 and iodine 131. Because these isotopes undergo a more rapid decay, observers had assumed that longer-lived isotopes like strontium 90 and cesium 137 constituted the only threat. However, experiments establish that radio-active substances do not remain in the stratosphere five to ten years, as the 1957 studies suggested, but rather from one to five years. Strontium 90, which is chemically similar to calcium concentrating in the bones and capable of producing bone cancer and leukemia, and cesium 137, which concentrates in the muscles and flesh and is capable of causing genetic damage to the hereditary cells, are still considered the greatest peril in nuclear fall-out. They take from twenty-eight to thirty years to lose half their radio-activity through decay. Nevertheless, the fact that fall-out from the stratosphere is more rapid than was assumed has undermined the belief that short-lived isotopes would lose their radio-activity before falling to earth.

Furthermore, some of these isotopes achieve selective concentration in a particular organ of the body, as with radio-active iodine and the thyroid. Had the test ban been maintained, the hazards from short-lived isotopes should have been negligible as they can be expected to decay and disappear. A more long-term danger arises from carbon 14 which according to recent findings has a radio-active half-life of 5,600 years. Surveys reveal that carbon 14 is produced by the bombardment of nitrogen in the atmosphere by the great flux of neutrons produced both by atomic and thermonuclear explosions. It is capable of producing damage equal to or exceeding other fall-out materials but spread over 1,000 years. However, over so extended a period, it is estimated that the continuous irradiation from natural sources maintained at its present rate will have even greater biological consequences than carbon 14.

In the face of the hazards, potential and real, of continued testing the case for maintaining the moratorium had seemed self-evident. Nevertheless, a government considering such a policy is confronted by at least four problems. The first, to which we shall return in conclusion, is the fact that disarmament historically is not the prelude, but the consequence, of relaxed international tensions. The second stems from the persistent Soviet opposition to general and unlimited on-site inspection and their demand for virtual self-inspection or at best limited international inspection coupled with the protection of the veto in any enforcement system. At one stage in the Geneva discussions, the Soviet delegate appeared to make further concessions but the subsequent deterioration of East-West relations prevented any firm testing of the genuineness of this policy shift.

The third results from new technical problems such as the fact that a U.S. nuclear explosion in the upper atmosphere is known to have gone undetected and the further discovery that underground tests of limited magnitude can be conducted without detection. History may record that both of these problems were met through technical and political developments, but, despite some advances in arms negotiations between the two sides at Geneva, they remained obstacles to an agreement.

The fourth is a product of the policies embraced by other states.

The resumption of testing by the Soviet Union left our leaders no choice but to consider the steps essential to preserving our relative nuclear power position in the struggle with the Soviet Union.

In surveying the facts concerning the problem of fall-out, this essay falls somewhere between the findings of alarmists and those seized by complacency. Because the picture is less immediately critical than some maintain, is scarcely cause for complacency. Yet political diagnosis depends on the dual evaluation of the facts and those alternative policies that both sides consider practical. No reasonable patient would argue that a surgeon should discard the laboratory findings of medical technicians. Similarly, a disarmament program urged on a statesman which in its essentials ran in the face of conclusions by military and political specialists seems doomed to failure. The facts are often many-sided, and no more than the surgeon can ignore complicating and contingent circumstances can the statesman hurry down the one way street of the crusader or the champion of the "simple answer." Here the patience of Job and the wisdom of Solomon are required.

Limited nuclear war

A second broad problem has its roots in the trend of modern states to modernize and streamline their limited war capacities through substitution of small nuclear weapons for conventional military hardware. Military experts in the United States and Western Europe argue that parity with the Russians is impossible in conventional land armies where the Soviet Union enjoys a substantial comparative advantage both in population and in ground forces in being. They insist that small, highly mobile task forces equipped with limited nuclear weapons are more efficient and less costly to support.

Apparently Western Europe would be the principal theater of operations in which limited nuclear forces could be effective. Vast areas in Asia and Africa are relatively immune to these weapons not only because land masses and population factors restrict their use but because of the far-reaching moral and political consequences. The response of newly emergent peoples to the nation that used them first could be a decisive factor in the present struggle. However, Europe is an area in which small nuclear weapons are considered by some to be practical.

It is argued that should war break out, both the Soviet Union and the United States would have a stake in keeping the outbreak of nuclear hostilities limited. At the point that the conflict deteriorated beyond this stage, particularly with intercontinental missiles being available, Soviet and American soil would come under fire. Moreover, Europeans whose twenty odd NATO divisions face several hundred Soviet divisions likewise have an interest in counteracting numbers with highly efficient, self-contained nuclear units capable of keeping the enemy constantly off balance by never allowing any consolidation of territorial gains and by wiping out heavy concentrations of forces.

Proponents of a limited nuclear war strategy argue further that their policies need not result in unusually heavy casualties in human lives. In both conventional and all-out nuclear war, cities and industrial centers become appropriate military targets. In limited war, however, armies with high mobility and self-sufficiency replace cities as prime targets. Missiles and vertical take-off aircraft can be widely dispersed and concealed so that the elimination of a few important airfields is no longer essential. Opposing military forces are more important than communication systems or industrial centers, for each unit to the extent it is self-contained is the depository of its own crucial weapons.

This trend of thought foresees built-in restrictions to widespread destruction. It envisages sanctuaries, including cities and strategic nuclear forces (e.g., SAC), that will be relatively immune to nuclear strikes by the enemy. It questions whether limited nuclear war would be as destructive as conventional warfare given this prospect of self-limitation. Finally it urges that military experts not be defeatist about limited nuclear war at a time when the entire planning and development of our military establishment is built around nuclear weapons. The West, because of its superior industrial potential and broader, more diversified technology stands to gain more than the antagonist from the development of limited nuclear capacities, provided it devotes itself to this task with real dedication. Our very qualities of personal initiative and mechanical aptitude favor the West if we are prepared to sacrifice personal comfort in the interest of public safety.

On the other hand, an equally responsible body of opinion has grave and serious doubts that a limited nuclear strategy is possible. It asks whether the terms themselves are not mutually contradictory. It points to the fact that modern war, whatever the state of technology, has not been limited in the past. Witness the bombing of civilian centers and merchant ships in World War II. It argues that tactical nuclear weapons are now available that exceed in destructiveness the bombs used at Hiroshima and Nagasaki. The use of limited nuclear weapons will set off a tragic cycle of increasing military commitments that will eventuate in all-out nuclear warfare. A conventional war has a clearly defined cut-off point but a war fought with low-yield nuclear weapons would tempt the losing side to redress the balance by introducing weapons of greater and greater power.

For the region that comprised the battlefield, a limited nuclear conflict would cause destruction that approximated an all-out thermonuclear war. Europe would scarcely applaud limited as against total war, for it could be laid waste by tactical no less than strategic nuclear weapons however preferable this might be for the peoples within Soviet or American territory. If the aim of American policy is to preserve the people and civilization of Western Europe, limited nuclear warfare is not the way to do it. Nor can our allies be expected to see such a policy as in their self-interest.

A limited nuclear war strategy is questioned on other grounds as well. Its critics point out that it would require more, not fewer forces. Supporting strength for highly modernized forces must be increased and more widely dispersed. Greater reserves in proportion to front-line troops must be available to provide for the higher ratio of casualties anticipated. Thus limited nuclear warfare is not cheaper in cost or manpower than limited conventional warfare at any level of effort. For these reasons, certain experts maintain that the United States and its NATO allies cannot overcome its relative weaknesses in manpower by this expedient without far-reaching sacrifices.

The issue between the proponents and the foes of a limited nuclear strategy can be resolved only if we clarify the purpose such capacities are intended to serve. There is at least reasonable doubt that such a strategy provides a short-cut to less painful military victory. However, agreement may be possible on another level. Specifically, NATO's capacity for limited nuclear warfare may be the sword to deter the Russians from using their nuclear weapons in a limited attack. Without such a deterrent, NATO countries might be more vulnerable to Soviet aggression. The Russians weighing the costs of introducing tactical nuclear weapons in a limited European war in which we lacked such capacity might conclude that the risks were negligible.

They might determine that they could quickly overrun European land armies. Similarly if our sole deterrent rested in strategic all-out re-taliation, they could conclude they would escape retaliation in kind. It is in these terms that a limited nuclear establishment probably has a rational basis as a deterrent even though it cannot be defended as the means of an easy victory in war.

Prospects for survival in nuclear war

Confronted with the specter of all-out war, President Dwight D. Eisenhower late in his second term summed up the dilemma in the phrase "there is no alternative to peace." The bombs dropped over Hiroshima and Nagasaki had an explosive equivalent of 20,000 tons TNT (20 kilotons). Thermonuclear devices are now available with an explosive equivalent of more than 50,000,000 tons TNT (50 megatons) and there is apparently no upper limit. A 20 megaton weapon possesses a lethal radius of 8 miles and its area of total destruction is 48 square miles. Within such an area, 75 per cent of the population would be killed and the remainder critically injured. The radio-active effects of such a device would spread over an area larger than the state of New Jersey. If the enemy launched a successful attack on fifty of our metropolitan centers, at least 40 per cent of the population, 50 per cent of key facilities and 60 per cent of industry would be critically damaged.

In the face of these appalling figures, many are tempted to throw up their hands in despair. It should be remembered, however, that even if as many as 90 million Americans were killed in the first strike of a pre-emptive attack, this would still leave 90 million people alive. Agencies like the RAND Corporation and the present Administration of the State of New York urge consideration of measures that might increase the number of survivors to 120 or 150 million people. Some evidence exists that non-military programs of civil defense could appreciably increase our capacity to survive an initial nuclear attack and restore the national economy and democratic institutions. Non-military defense measures would of course depend on the effectiveness of both strategic-offense and active-defense capabilities. The latter would involve the "hardening" and dispersal of U.S. nuclear resources. It would require the strengthening of polaris and inter-continental guided missile capabilities and the development of more effective anti-missile devices. Any responsible U.S. government must weigh and evaluate the costs and possible effectiveness of its strategic offensive, air defense and local-war forces.

Nevertheless, within these limits, non-military defense is theoretically possible. Radiation meters within improvised fall-out shelters can guide decontamination work and indicate when it is safe to come out of shelters. A RAND study indicates that: "With no non-military defense measures, a completely effective 150-city attack could result in 160 million deaths in the United States. . . . With a system of fall-out shelters, and given several hours' warning . . . casualties might be reduced to 60 million. With a complete system of blast and fall-out shelters, and even with only 30 to 60 minutes of warning, casualties might be held to 25 million."[1] Less warning might increase the casualties while prior strategic evacuation could reduce casualties still further. These estimates presuppose not that people would occupy the shelters permanently but that they would use them under an effective warning system.

Moreover, costs would probably not be prohibitive. Suitably located mines might be adapted for both blast and fall-out protection at an estimated cost for emergency 7-day occupancy of $25-$35 per person. Light shelters for 90-day occupancy (food, bedrolls, cold rations, latrines, etc.) might cost $150 per person and corrugated steel shelters buried deep in the earth could be built in the form of bunkroom accommodations for 90-day occupancy for from $300-$400 per person. One engineering firm estimates that a system of deep rock shelters under Manhattan Island for 4 million people could be provided at a cost of $500-$700 per person. While more research is needed before definitive answers are possible, prospects are sufficiently promising to warrant further thought and attention. The proposals of President Kennedy in his message of May 25, 1961, envisage the initial use and strengthening of existing public buildings appropriate for non-military defense and go beyond individual responsibility for unit defense.

In other fields, prior planning and organized efforts would serve at least to ease the catastrophe. Agricultural products in storage as a result of price-support operations would be sufficient to supply a diet of 2000 calories per day to 180 million people for more than a year. These stocks are sufficiently dispersed to make them largely invulnerable to a city attack and after appropriate milling any grain including crops close to harvesting could be made suitable as an emergency ration. The cost of 3 months' shelter rations for 180 million people would be $6-$7 billion plus storage and deterioration costs. Adjustment of crop patterns and land use after a 50-city attack should permit a safe recuperation of agricultural production.

Most observers assume that industry would be more vulnerable than agriculture at least under existing patterns of industrial concentration. The fifty largest American cities contain only one-third the total population but more than one-half of manufacturing capital. What could be produced outside the 50 destroyed cities in the first year after reorganization? One study suggests that surviving capital could permit a Gross National Product of 50-60 per cent of the pre-attack GNP. On a per capita basis, if 85 per cent of the population survived, this would mean a level comparable to that of 1929 or 1940. A further estimate suggests that the pre-attack GNP could be achieved in a decade. Industrial recovery would of course depend on such things as stockpiling in peace of construction materials for patching up partially damaged capital, sheltering normal inventories of metals, building materials and machinery, and sheltering complete plants or standby components of plants in the durable goods sector.

We have no intention of minimizing the disaster of a thermonuclear war nor of disparaging the importance of continuous efforts at arms control by suggesting that perhaps there exist more promising means of alleviating the tragedy than has been generally recognized. Nevertheless the areas we have mentioned are but a few of the important spheres within which responsible authorities advise that prospects of survival could be brighter than sometimes assumed. Resonable men differ on many of these issues and a broad research, development and planning program would be necessary before more general and authoritative estimates could be made. In addition, experts in the government and the RAND Corporation tell us the means are at hand to limit the long-term biological damage to the population from total radiation and of enforcing counter-measures to contain the strontium 90 problem even after very large attacks. If we assume disaster could never strike or fatalistically rule out well-laid responses to catastrophe, the alleviation of the tragedy will be impossible.

The search for disarmament and arms control

No matter how assiduously states prepare for military and non-military defense, the ever-increasing menace of nuclear disaster remains. The weight and expansion of armament capacities add to the general tension. The Soviet Union has proposed a single formula of general and complete disarmament in four years. On March 21, 1961, a new American delegation led by Mr. Arthur Dean along with British and Soviet representatives resumed negotiations at Geneva on a treaty to ban the testing of nuclear weapons. A new approach was called for and a task force under John J. McCloy undertook a comprehensive study. In Secretary of State Dean Rusk's words: "The matter needs a fresh and imaginative review by all concerned." The administration had no illusions about "the dismal history of man's attempts to lay down his arms" but it sought to chart a course enabling men "to move from endless discussion to practical steps—small steps if necessary, large steps if possible." One practical step that assuredly would not end the arms race but might lead to more significant measures was a test ban. The administration's approach was a pragmatic one testing out Soviet intentions in areas of most probable immediate common interest.

This approach falls midway between the two prevailing viewpoints on disarmament in modern society. On the one extreme, many of the most sensitive and noble spirits believe that disarmament and peace are synonymous. History is the melancholy record of states locked in deadly rivalry driven by the haunting fear that a stronger neighbor threatens them and striving for security through ever-increasing armaments. War is the result of an arms race spiralling upwards until weapons which can no longer be hoarded are used. "The one thing you cannot do with bayonets is sit on them."

The evidence is clear that the new administration categorically rejects this interpretation of history. The President's disarmament adviser declared on February 25, 1961: "History shows that some wars can arguably be traced to a preceding arms race, and it shows that others can be as clearly related to disarmament and bad faith rather than armament." Democracies have a penchant for tempting thieves. They are often the last to arm and, like the shopkeeper who leaves his goods on the street exposed to all the natural and human elements, may invite crime and aggression. As Secretary of State Rusk observed:

> Our history shows a democracy's deep reluctance to bear arms in times of peace—to the point where we have learned that weakness, too, can be a danger. After World War II, for example, we demobilized until we had no division and no air group ready for combat.

Our defense budget was one-fourth of its present level. The rebuild-
ing of our strength was a necessity undertaken reluctantly, forced
upon us by those who would not join in building a peaceful world.

At the opposite extreme of the spectrum, opponents of continued
disarmament talks urge that the free nations at most make one final
effort to negotiate an arms agreement. They point to the endless
round of discussions, the volumes of reports and studies, and the
many fruitless months and years of futile negotiations. Why not
bring matters to a head, force a showdown and, failing agreement,
shore up every support of the garrison state and prepare for the
worst? The responsible leader must ask himself "is this fulfilling my
trust?" He must brood over Robert Oppenheimer's warning that in
all-out thermonuclear conflict the only issue will be whether there
are sufficient survivors to bury the dead. He must ask whether diplomacy by ultimatum holds out hope for the future. He must measure
his actions by our commitment through the United Nations Charter
to disarmament as a solemn purpose. Finally, he must consider
whether the example we wish to set for others at a time when some
are proposing regional arms limitations is of a great power withdraw-
ing from the field. If we abandon the search for limitation of armaments, will those who are considering limiting military preparations
to arms essential to internal security purposes resume pursuit of the
arms race on every front?

The progress of the Geneva talks has hardly been encouraging. On
April 18, 1961, the West which since October 31, 1958, through 292
meetings had endeavored to negotiate an agreement on a piecemeal
basis introduced a complete test ban proposal. Their draft treaty
would provide for banning all nuclear testing in the atmosphere,
under water and in space. Underground tests of weapons smaller than
the Hiroshima bomb were to be dealt with by a separate moratorium
pending research on a foolproof detection system. Inspection teams
would not include nationals of the country to be inspected, although
there are signs this point might be negotiable. Inspections numbering
twenty annually would be conducted in the Soviet Union, the United
States and Britain and her dependencies. The Soviets have consistently
maintained that inspection was merely a cover for espionage activities
by the West within Russian boundaries. The Soviet proposal, therefore, has been for three inspections annually and while the West has

shown itself prepared to reduce their present requirement of 20 inspections to 12, it would be unlikely to accept the Soviet plan. The basic issue over inspection has been, of course, the reluctance of a closed society to accept incursions into its society when it had little to gain from inspections within the open territory of a free adversary.

A more serious and unexpected issue arises from Soviet demands for a veto over all inspection. Walter Lippmann in reporting an interview with Premier Khrushchev in the Spring of 1961 noted:

> He would never accept a single neutral administration. Why? Because, he said, while there are neutral countries, there are no neutral men . . . I will never entrust the security of the Soviet Union to a foreigner.

In place of a single neutral adminstrator to administer the treaty, the Soviets propose a three-man council. It had been agreed in talks at Geneva in 1960 that a commission would be established made up of two Russians, two Westerners and three officials from neutral countries. At the same time, the Russians had agreed there should be a single neutral administrator for this control commission. Then the Soviets, in the same way they rejected the authority of the U. N. Secretary General, overturned an earlier agreement and demanded in effect a veto-at-will over any inspection procedure.

Speculation over the shift in Soviet policy is probably pointless. The observer is tempted to ask whether continued successes in outer space and growing influence in the Western Hemisphere and the non-Western world has led to a less conciliatory stand. Whatever the forces to which Soviet leaders are responding, hopes and expectations of a test ban have been appreciably dampened.

But the new position may be merely the latest Soviet tactic in the cold war. Beyond that, the West may not have exhausted the alternatives open to it by discussions at Geneva. What are the prospects for reductions of armaments within countries other than the great powers? Is there a chance that East and West might thin out their forces in areas such as central and Eastern Europe? What hopes can we reasonably entertain that Western Europe might increasingly provide for its own security within Europe except for protection through the ultimate threat of nuclear deterrence and retaliation from this side of the Atlantic? Could negotiations on armament reduction of this order be linked more closely with efforts to ameliorate political tensions? What of the relations between arms talks and the problem of Germany? When and how can or should the United Nations be drawn into the sphere of arms reduction?

The resumption of nuclear tests by the Soviet Union on the eve of the Belgrade Conference of non-committed states shattered the illusions of moralists and neutrals alike. Many of us in the past, in lecturing American policy-makers on concessions that the United States should make, have failed to grasp the nature of the Soviet threat. When the Soviet Union sees that its relative power position can be strengthened through steps such as the resumption of tests, it will act irrespective of the judgment of world public opinion. An ethic of protest that admonishes western leaders alone without recognizing this fact, is in the end an ethic of irresponsibility. An ethic of responsibility by contrast must accept the fact that the contest with Soviet Russia will not end through a single dramatic act. It seems destined to continue throughout the present generation with the ebb and flow of successive intensifications and reductions of tensions. The struggle can perhaps be limited and contained, the means of violence restricted or reduced, the scale and temper of conflict checked and circumscribed, and deterrents be made more credible. We are doomed not to extinction but to living with dangers more terrifying than man has ever known, at least for the forseeable future. I am persuaded that the moralist must help prepare men to live under these circumstances, not merely beckon him to a happier if imaginary land. We need moral resources not alone to be firm or flexible but to be both in dealings with Soviet leaders. There will be times as in the autumn of 1961, when firmness must precede flexibility if the adversary is to resume serious negotiations. But there may also be moments in history when from a position of strength, the West must be ready to initiate new and more flexible proposals for peace. To sense these moments and seize them at their tide is the ultimate challenge of statesmanship. No one calling from the sidelines can solve the problem of timing: when to act and when to wait, when to be firm and when to be flexible, or when to resist and when to negotiate. Yet success or failure in this endlessly complicated and uncertain process, far more than exhortations or blueprints of utopia will bring peace or war to the tormented human race.

It may be that we shall flounder and make little progress on armaments until we ask the proper question. Foreign policy to a considerable degree lies in posing the right question. Once the right question is posed, the answer comes more nearly within reach. It may be that this question is "can we negotiate a viable test ban safeguarded by essential provisions for inspection?" But even if success should elude our negotiators for the present here, there may be other "small steps" that will yield more readily to discussion. The phrase "one final attempt to reach agreement" is seldom helpful in diplomacy. Or arms agreements may await innovations or controls yet to be thrown up by the shifting waves of history. In this field, we may be awaiting new concepts, procedures or institutions. The need to adapt swiftly to new environmental factors invites us to reflect on the words of Alfred North Whitehead in his *Adventures of Ideas*:

> Tradition is warped by the vicious assumption that each generation will substantially live amid the conditions governing the lives of its fathers, and will transmit those conditions to mold with equal force the lives of its children. We are living in the first period of human history for which this assumption is false.
>
> In the past the time span of important changes was considerably longer than that of a single human life—today this time span is considerably shorter than that of human life, and accordingly our training must prepare individuals to face a novelty of conditions.

The novelty of conditions in a thermonuclear age is the ultimate challenge to the wit of man. The urgency of the crisis with which all men are confronted by the utter destructiveness of the new instruments of warfare calls for imagination, prudence and vision. Those who hope for prompt and simple answers in approaches to disarmament will not be comforted by a recitation of these truths nor will the cynics or the utopians. Yet for those who strive gallantly and continually to meet the problems of each new day, this almost unbearable crisis could bring their finest hour.

NOTE

1. RAND "Report on a Study of Non-Military Defense," July 1, 1958, p. 12.

Moral urgencies
in the nuclear context

BY JOHN C. BENNETT

I AM writing this chapter against the background of Christian ethics. It is fortunate that there is much overlapping on social ethics between the minds of Christians and Jews and those, who without any traditional religious allegiance, are committed to a sensitive humanistic ethic. A person must write out of the particular commitments and backgrounds of his own thought however much he may recognize and rejoice in this overlapping. I want to make clear that on none of the ethical judgments in this chapter do Christians have a monopoly and that these judgments are so intertwined with prudential judgments and interpretations of the changing world situation that there would be disagreement about most of them among Christians.

There is a deep and harrassing problem whenever we try to relate any sensitive and universal ethic to the behavior of nations. There are no Christian nations or states and there is no Christian foreign policy. Yet Christians are citizens and they must choose between national policies and often they are in positions where they have direct responsibility for the making of policy. In each nation there is a Christian Church which retains that name only as it is part of a universal Church and so the member of a Church has in fact a dual citizenship and he recognizes an ultimate loyalty to the God whom the Church worships and not to any nation or state. And whatever he may believe to be the will of God about any particular situation, he knows that God cares for the welfare and dignity of the people of all nations, including nations which may be adversaries of his own nation, that he is a God of righteousness and mercy under whose judgment all nations are convicted of egoism and pride and hardness of heart. And in particular, under his judgment, the nations that have idealistic national purposes are seen to be inclined to a self-righteousness that distorts their view of other nations.

Since there are no Christian nations or states, Christian citizens should recognize the special functions of the state as trustee for the interests and security of a particular nation and should not ask the state to act as though it were a Church or a Christian state. The policy maker and the citizen must decide and act with a realistic estimate of

93

the possibilities that are available to him in his role within the situation. There are limits to those possibilities set by the self-interest of man, especally of political man, but there are also particular limits set by past choices, by the particular configuration of the history of one's own time. Churches and Christian citizens can do much to make the nation more aware of the humanity and the needs of all persons affected by national policy and they can help the nation to be self-critical to some degree at the points of its greatest temptation. Christian love with its ultimate claims transcends what is possible for nations as nations but there is a wisdom in it concerning the solidarity of humanity which even nations can learn. Christian repentance cannot be expected of a nation but again there is a wisdom in it concerning the common sin of all men and concerning national pride and hardness of heart from which even nations can profit.

The conflict between Christian ethics and national policy has always been very conspicuous in the whole area of armaments and international war. So obvious has been this conflict that in all centuries some Christians have felt called to renounce all involvement in the political life of nations at those points that are closest to the war-making policies and powers of the state. While in detail it may be difficult to draw this line, there has been a very impressive pacifist witness against war and preparations for war throughout Christian history. The dominant Christian traditions have opposed this solution of the problem. They have not been able to justify an absolute law against military action by the state because at times this has seemed to be the only alternative to surrender to oppressive forms of power, but undoubtedly there has been a tendency to be far too complacent about war and this has come in part from the fact that Churches have reflected the national culture and the majority opinion of the citizens and they have often been close allies of the state. After full allowance has been made for these popular distortions of Christian judgment there has been a strong case on Christian grounds for the use of force to defend men against tyranny. There is a difference between those forms of the Christian ethic which identify Christian love with a particular law of non-violence and those which insist that Christian love must in each set of circumstances seek to serve the greater good and to avoid the greater evil. In seeking to avoid the greater evil the power of states is often a necessary instrument.

In the chapters by both John Herz and Paul Ramsey there is emphasis on the fact that in the past the use of violence in war has been limited by various factors. Most of these have been morally neutral but, as Ramsey insists, there has been a Christian conscience at work in the limitation of war. Modern Catholicism has inherited a tradition of the "just war" that is just partly because of definite limitations in the use of violence. But this has been a broad Christian tradition supported, it must be admitted, by the technology of war in earlier periods. As the technology of war has changed there has been no adequate wrestling with the problem of what this means for the Christian ethic of war. The difficulty has been compounded by the fact that in our time the alternative to the use of increasingly destructive weapons has seemed to be surrender to totalitarian tyranny. In the Second World War, as I shall emphasize later, American Christians gradually became accustomed to all of the violence that the development of the technology of weapons made possible.

Today Christians and other morally sensitive citizens in the United States are in a peculiarly difficult position because of the concentrated responsibility that goes with its power. A citizen of Denmark or India or even Britain or indeed of any nation that does not have the chance of possessing decisive nuclear power is spared many immediate difficult decisions though he may still feel related to them because his own destiny may depend on them. American citizens have concentrated responsibility. What they do or leave undone may have a direct effect on whether or not the world moves toward nuclear war or on whether or not it lays itself open to Communist pressures which might shift the balance of most kinds of power in favor of Communism. Their moral commitments and sensitivities are deeply involved on both sides of this terrible dilemma.

For a decade I was able to live with this dilemma without too great inner disturbance. I was convinced that the only threat to peace was from Communist aggression and that our nuclear deterrent power would prevent such aggression and thus keep the peace. In 1950 I was able to sign the Dun Report on "The Christian Conscience and Weapons of Mass Destruction", which refused to say that we would not use the hydrogen bomb first in a war because I believed that the surest way of preventing the war in which it might be used anyway was to keep the adversary guessing as to whether or not we might use it in response to a conventional attack on western Europe. Of course everyone knew that there were some risks in emphasizing the deterrent effect of nuclear weapons to this extent but the risk seemed small compared with any alternative policy that was politically or psychologically possible.

Today the dilemma is much more difficult to live with because I do not have the same confidence that the deterrent during the next decade will prevent the war. Something more is called for than the preservation of the "balance of terror." For a few years longer it may still be effective but if the nuclear arms race continues for a decade with no controls upon it, there is far too much danger that war will come from a technical accident, from a miscalculation of the adversary's intention or from the extension of a limited military operation to a general nuclear war.

The chapter by Dr. Herz emphasizes all of these dangers which may become more threatening every year. They make it morally imperative to have fresh thoughts about the relationship between the two generally recognized objectives of national policy: the protection of as large an area of freedom in the world as possible and the prevention of nuclear war. In the past, the tendency has been to accent the first objective and to assume that the deterrent designed to prevent Communist aggression would also prevent the war. Today there is greater need of independent concern for the prevention of the war. Also, so long as we assumed that the possession of the nuclear bombs would prevent their use, we could avoid the hardest questions. Now we must face the ultimate ethical issue involved in their use.

I think that we should rule out the short-cut of unilateral nuclear disarmament. I am not sure that, if this were psychologically or politically possible, it would necessarily invite aggression. It might be such a shock to the world that it would start a quite unexpected beneficent chain reaction. But no government that has the responsibility for American security and more broadly for preserving the security of the "free world" could act on the basis of such a hopeful possibility. Granting that there are risks either way, I doubt if Christian citizens should urge their government to take the more obvious risk of permitting such a monopoly of power to develop on the other side. There is the added consideration that at this stage the chances of an agreement on multilateral disarmament may be greater if there is approximate equality of power to be scaled down on both sides.

The growth of nuclear pacifism in this period seems to me to be natural and it is probably no accident that it has greater strength in Britain, Germany and Japan than in the United States because those countries have less direct responsibility for preventing a nuclear monopoly in the Communist world. The nuclear pacifists must have their own second best policy which they would recommend to the United States government in the light of the fact that there is no possibility that the administration, the Congress or the general public would support a pacifist policy. On the other hand, the concentration of responsibility for military defense in this nation always is in danger of causing us to become too preoccupied with the maintenance of military power and of our failing to see aspects of the situation which both nuclear pacifists and the nations that have more detachment because they have less power can see more clearly than we.

Some experts on the problems of nuclear warfare emphasize the possibilities of reducing the destructive consequences of nuclear war, if it should take place. This is the theme of the very powerful book by Dr. Herman Kahn, *On Thermonuclear War*,[1] a book that is easily caricatured as it seeks to make the prospect of nuclear war tolerable. Kahn writes against those who talk about the effects of nuclear war as involving annihilation or total destruction of the nation or of the race. He points out that a war may result in the death of forty million Americans but that it is a real gain if the figure is not eighty million. He writes to urge the kind of preparations that might enable the United States to reduce the number of dead in a war and to preserve as much of the capacity for national recuperation as possible. There are, however, four criticisms of his actual portrayal of the consequences of nuclear war which, if sound, prevent Kahn's approach from giving us any real relief from the moral pressure of the nuclear dilemma.

Kahn's picture of the difference between the nation before and after a nuclear war is entirely quantitative. He may be right that there will be 140,000,000 survivors after such a war, though his view of the actual physical conditions under which they survive may be too optimistic. Just what kind of terrain they will move out of their shelters to occupy is quite uncertain. But the greatest lack in this book is any consideration of the more intangible effects of a nuclear war. What will happen to the emotional health or morale of the people, to the structures of community, to the quality of life, to the institutions of freedom? His perfunctory answers to such questions as these show that they are not taken seriously.

Here I appeal from Herman Kahn with his show of tough realism to the mature realism of Hans Morgenthau who says of Kahn's estimates of the chances of national recovery after a full scale nuclear war that only one who is "possessed not only by an extreme optimism but by an almost unthinking faith" can believe "that civilization, any civilization, Western or otherwise, could survive such an unprecedented catastrophe." Professor Morgenthau adds: "The fundamental error in the reasoning to which I am referring, it seems to me, lies in the assumption that the moral fiber of a civilization has an unlimited capacity to recover from shock."[2]

A second weakness in Kahn's argument is that it presupposes very extensive and almost ideally organized civilian defense which provides bomb shelters for most citizens, an adequate supply of food and water and other necessities in the right place at the right time, preparations for the evacuation of many cities (inhabitants of New York have a right to be pessimistic about this but they probably belong to the expendable 40,000,000 anyway). Given a radiation meter each family will emerge from its shelter prepared to face a world of unknown hazards. This kind of civil defense planning is probably psychologically and politically impossible in this country. The kind of synchronized preparation for such a variety of unfamiliar threats and deficiencies (including the deficiency of not-too-contaminated air in the shelters) that is required here would call for a more prescient and efficient government at all levels than has ever been known in this country. It would call for a change in the lives of all citizens long before the projected disaster which it is difficult for me to imagine. It would call for an enormous increase of expenditures which would itself involve a great political hurdle. Such civil defense would stimulate inventions that might soon make it obsolete and in itself become a factor in the arms race. It would have to overcome not only much of the individualism of the American people but also a deep feeling that it is unlikely to be effective enough to be worth the cost. But it would also have to overcome a moral revulsion which supports in a vague way this shrinking from the enterprise based upon common sense. This kind of civil defense, if it is thorough enough to be effective, would itself be so dehumanizing that rejection of it might be a part of a broad moral rejection of a nuclear deformation of humanity. Whatever may be said in principle about this moral rejection of such thorough civil defense there is a strong case for the moral protest against lesser civil defense measures which are in fact highly deceptive concerning the realities of nuclear war. I recognize the right and duty of the state to do what can be done for the security of its citizens. But it should not do little things in such a way as to lull them into a false sense of security. But such reflections are not a part of the argument. The important point is that Kahn's projections presuppose a program of civil defense which is of quite a different order from any now envisaged and it is doubtful if it is psychologically or politically possible.

A third defect in Herman Kahn's whole approach is that he did "not look at the interaction among the effects we did study."[3] Pages 90-92 of this crucially important book give one pause concerning the reliability of the whole. Kahn, for example, speaks of the destruction of fifty or so major metropolitan areas of the country and then proceeds to discuss the possibilities of recovery on the assumption that a reconstruction program is "not complicated by social disorganization, loss of personnel, radioactivity and so forth."[4] And then he says: "But if all these things happened together and all the other effects were added at the same time, one cannot help but have some doubts." All of the show of technical knowledge of weaponry and strategy do not make up for such basic lack of wisdom as these words suggest. How would personnel not be lost and how would surviving personnel get to the places where it would be needed?

A fourth limitation of this whole type of argument is that it is related only to the present stage of the technology of weapons. Kahn himself is very pessimistic about what might be true of nuclear war in the late 1960's and early 1970's. Indeed it should be said that he is a strong advocate of arms control because of his fears of a later stage of the arms race. In the following passage we see clearly how limited the relevance of his discussion really is: "Since I further believe that in the pre-1965 period, possibly extending into the late 60s or early 70s, it will be possible (if proper preparations have been made) to still have a country after most wars, we should make those preparations."[5]

As I have said, it is quite legitimate to study ways and means to enable a nation to survive a thermonuclear attack. The unfortunate aspect of this approach to the subject is that it has the effect of making light of the full range of consequences of such an attack. As William L. Miller says of Herman Kahn's book: "Therefore treatments like this badly need a corrective and criticism of a larger frame, in which military strategy is subordinated to politics and politics connected to ethics, in a human and humane rather than a mathematical language." Dr. Miller goes on to say that Kahn "does not enough admit the possibility, that by making thermonuclear war seem thinkable and survival possible one may make thermonuclear war more likely. The tender-mindedness he wishes to overcome may be a basic moral revulsion that should not be overcome."[6]*

II

I shall now present several considerations about nuclear war and about the nuclear arms race which are very much neglected in current discussion.

It would be less than candid if I did not admit a real difficulty that I feel in writing this part of the chapter. If the points that I shall now make should be greatly emphasized in our country, the effect might be some lessening of the power and the capacity for maneuver of the United States and other nations which are seeking to balance the power of the Communist nations. One could feel less inner conflict about this matter if there were in the Soviet Union and China freedom for this kind of utterance. I believe, however, that those who share the views which I shall present should not keep silent even though what they say may have some undesired effects. We are dealing with a dilemma. If we cover up the depth of the problem on one side of this dilemma, there is certain to be a measure of blindness to this side in our policy. I believe that there is now a tendency to cover up the realities and that thinking about policy is now to some extent blind to this side of the dilemma.

The kinds of moral warnings and sensitivities which I shall emphasize ought to be and often are part of the inner life of those who make military policy. But this is not likely to be the case for long if nothing is ever said about these moral considerations on their own terms, if they are left to the unexpressed private consciences of policy makers and other citizens. Also, I believe that if all who hold such views as I shall express were silent, we would all come to live in a very distorted moral universe. We might be able to deal more effectively with one aspect of the current situation, but we might be quite unprepared to deal with

* For a different emphasis, see Thompson, pp. 82-84.

the more human aspects of our present problems or with the next situation which we may have to face. Also, what are we to say about the function of those who within the Christian Church have a responsibility to keep alive a religious and moral witness which must not be trimmed to fit the exigencies of western strategy? It is not religiously or morally possible within such a context to remain silent.

1. *We must not deceive ourselves into believing that we could ever justify the use of megaton bombs for massive attacks on the centers of population of another country no matter what the provocation.* We could not justify retaliatory attacks which involve making good on a threat of deterrence. If we allowed ourselves to consent in advance to such attacks we would betray the best in our religious and moral traditions. There is justification for our having the retaliatory force to be directed against the striking power of the adversary and I shall deal with this later. Let it be granted that if we were attacked and if our missiles or bombers immediately began their flight to the great cities of the attacking nation, there might be little chance for self-recrimination. The survivors on both sides would be part of an overwhelming tragedy, and confrontation with a world of horror would leave calculations concerning more or less guilt rather irrelevant. The need of healing and forgiveness on all sides and the need of religious support for the day's life would be primary. But it is quite another thing to base the policy of a nation now on the expectation of total attacks against the people of another nation. How can a nation live with its conscience and know that it is preparing to kill twenty million children in another nation if the worst should come to the worst? We cannot be true to ourselves if we plan on the assumption that there are no moral limits in warfare, that military necessity is the ultimate law of life when the chips are down.

There has been little discussion of this issue and I am sure that one reason is that we have expected the deterrent to prevent the war in which the issue might arise. Also there is a feeling, as I have suggested, that if such things as these are said, the deterrent might be less effective. It is supposed that, if we say nothing about these ultimate problems, we have the best chance of preventing them from ever becoming our problems. For a few years it was possible to maintain this policy of silence but as the years become decades it cannot be done. This is all the more

true when we reflect on the reasons for believing that the deterrent cannot be counted on indefinitely to prevent the war.

There is another reason for the prevailing silence on the whole question of moral limits in time of war. Since the middle of the Second
World War there has been a gradual abdication of moral judgment
in relation to all military decisions. With the saturation bombing of
German and Japanese cities, long before the bombing of Hiroshima
and Nagasaki, Americans came to accept the idea that there are no
limits to the evil that may be done to the enemy at a distance. In the
early stages of this process of moral abdication there were some protests by the Churches. A Commission was formed by the Federal
Council of Churches under the chairmanship of Dr. Robert Calhoun
to discuss the problems of divine providence and of moral decisions
connected with war.[7] This commission did say that military necessity
could never be the ultimate standard but, because of the threat of a
Hitler victory, it was divided on the issue of obliteration bombing.
It did at a later time condemn the dropping of the atomic bombs on
Hiroshima and Nagasaki. In general we seem to have moved by
stages into the position that anything is permitted at a distance, while
there are still moral limits in the treatment of prisoners or other individuals close at hand. We could shrug off or even sanction the
killing of a hundred thousand people, mostly civilians, in a single
raid on Dresden or Hamburg or Tokyo, but we still would refrain
from sanctioning the torture of one individual whom we could
face as a person. There was a deterioration of our moral judgment
under the pressure of war. The technological momentum of weapons
outran our moral imagination. That momentum continues and the
pressure of the cold war has kept us from recovering our moral
balance.*

---

* More recently there has developed a common assumption that we should be
willing to initiate "a nuclear exchange" if we are threatened by defeat in the
use of conventional weapons in the neighborhood of Berlin. Doubtless the use of
tactical nuclear weapons is first in view but the likelihood of escalation into the
use of H-bombs against population centers is so great that a nation that initiates
the nuclear phase of a war takes upon itself an awful burden of guilt. Surely
in the case of Berlin one of the early results would be the destruction of the very
city which we would be seeking to save. In the whole discussion of the possible
initiation of the nuclear phase of the war the moral issue is seldom mentioned;
this is discussed as though it were chiefly a matter of strategy.

It may be argued that anyone who says what I have just said must inevitably advocate unilateral nuclear disarmament. I have already given my view that at the present time this is not psychologically or politically possible and that, because it would leave a monopoly of the decisive form of military power in the Communist world, it would not be desirable. There is an interim situation which does provide a basis for the possession of nuclear armament. What I have said against attacks on the centers of population in another country does not apply to attacks or threatened attacks on the striking power of that country. As I have suggested, this may be an interim situation. The effort of each nation is to make its retaliatory force invulnerable. This can be done to a considerable extent through hardening the bases or using submarines as bases and in other ways. It is often assumed by experts on strategy that the most desirable of all possible situations is one in which the retaliatory forces on both sides are so invulnerable that neither side will be tempted to attack the other because it cannot in advance destroy its retaliatory force. This is said to be a stable situation because it is based upon the ultimate in mutual deterrence. The difficulty is that even if such a situation were in existence, it is not sure how long it would last with changes in technology or with the appearance of other nuclear powers. Also, none of the systems of deterrence are likely to hold if a limited war should start in some part of the world and if in a time of panic a nation were tempted to strike out against the enemy's heartland. As one reads the books by the most cold-blooded experts on strategy it often seems that they presuppose a degree of rationality under stress that calls for almost as much faith as the optimism of idealists who presuppose virtue in all men. If limited war should take the form of a limitation of targets for nuclear attack to the enemy's bases, there is always the danger that the fall-out would be a disaster for the civilian population.

There may be a stage in which war will be postponed by the possession of invulnerable retaliatory forces on both sides. But the effect of this development on military planning is to make almost inevitable preparation to attack the centers of population in the nation that is feared. A retaliatory attack that is required by the whole scheme of deterrence would have to be an attack on the other nation's will to continue the war by the destroying of its people. Henry Kissinger in his *The Necessity for Choice*[8] says that already there is a tendency on the part of our military planners to think of our retaliatory force as designed "not so much to destroy the strategic power of the opponent as to threaten his social substance." Those are cold words but they raise the most acute moral problem in all of our thinking about nuclear war.

Those who go as far as to say what I have said in this chapter but who do not advocate unilateral nuclear disarmament must have great sympathy for the dilemmas of those who have responsibility for military planning. The efforts of many of them to shift the emphasis from nuclear weapons and "massive retaliation" to conventional arms and to a capability for limited military operations deserve praise. Also, it must be recognized that any discriminating use of nuclear arms that avoids attacks on centers of population may call for more rather than less capacity and especially more rather than less effective means of delivery. I say these things to myself especially, because my own temptation is to lose patience with the concerns of those who are responsible for military planning. And as I say them, I feel more strongly than ever the interim nature of this kind of discussion. If nuclear war is to be prevented, it will be necessary to find a way out of the present stalemate before many years have passed and if nuclear war comes we are sure to be faced with the moral dilemmas which I have emphasized.

The reader will detect a similarity between the view presented in these paragraphs and those which Dr. Ramsey elaborates with such power in his chapter. I agree with him that there is a distinction in emphasis between the armed forces of a nation and the civilian population though, as he explains, this is not, as far as adults are concerned, a moral difference. I have not put as much emphasis on this distinction because in practice there may be great difficulty in applying it except in a very broad way. His own use of the principle of the "double effect" of an action and his emphasis on the *intention* of the attack on a military target opens the way for the permissible killing of vast numbers of civilians in a war, for more and more as the destructive power of the weapons increase. If we do admit the moral possibility of "counter-forces" warfare as he and I both do, the danger is that this may too easily become a sanction for the wholesale killing of the people of another nation if the large bombs are used at all. For this reason I think that it is useful to be guided not only by intention but also by a realistic view of the total consequences of an attack. On the basis of intention almost any degree of destruction can be rationalized. To prevent this I should also consider such tests of destructiveness as the effect on the fabric of community and on the capacity for recuperation. I grant that these are vague but they can perhaps be made more precise. As Ramsey insists, it is the human beings about whom we must be concerned. But the human beings who happen to be drafted into the armed forces and who share the same purposes and the same helplessness to influence events as the civilian populations need also to be considered. To repress them and the force which they bear is a necessity, not because they are more guilty or less human but because such repression is the direct way to reduce violence. But wholesale destruction of the personnel in the armed forces is also a moral problem that should not be neglected.*

2. *We need to take more seriously than we do the effect of large-scale nuclear war on the quality of life in the surviving community.* Herman Kahn has a chapter entitled: "Will the survivors envy the dead?" but he is quite facile in coming to the conclusion that they need not do so. But even under this title, he deals chiefly in quantitative terms. Robert Oppenheimer has posed the quantitative question when he asks if there will be enough survivors to bury the dead?[9] Both of these questions keep us in touch with the realities of nuclear war.

Destruction of wealth might reach a point at which society would be reduced to barbarism, not primarily because of the material deprivations in themselves, but because the survivors might find themselves engaged in a primitive struggle for the means of subsistence. Such catastrophes may produce a few saints and heroes but they can lead to the brutalization of the common life. The discussion of the use of guns to protect one's shelter space and one's supply of food against hordes of neighbors is a grim pre-view of the likely break-down of community after a nuclear attack.

* As the editor of this volume, I have felt that I should not generally argue in this chapter with my fellow contributors. It happens that Dr. Ramsey's chapter and mine have grown out of earlier papers and we formed the habit of arguing with each other on marginal issues and this fact explains the criticisms of my position in Dr. Ramsey's chapter.

Reinhold Niebuhr has recently suggested one intangible factor which is usually neglected in the discussion of the effects of nuclear war on a civilization and that is what he calls "the monstrous guilt" that would be incurred in such a war.[10] This might have the effect of morally destroying a civilization. Such a consideration does not enter at all into the usual calculations.

The urgencies in such a postwar situation would make it very difficult for institutions of freedom to survive. Since the present world conflict and the present nuclear arms race is seen on our side to be for the sake of freedom, it would be ironical if freedom itself proved to be a casualty of the war. I do not say that it would never rise again but the sober words of Herbert Butterfield are probably nearer the truth than the exhortations of those who, seeing only the danger of Communism, would support policies which might lead to the loss of freedom through war. Butterfield writes: "With modern weapons we could easily put civilization back a thousand years, while the course of a single century can produce a colossal transition from despotic regimes to a system of liberty."[11]

Walter Lippmann has emphasized the extent to which a nuclear war would probably destroy the institutions of freedom. He says: "It would be followed by a savage struggle for existence as the survivors crawled out of their shelters, and the American republic would be replaced by a stringent military dictatorship trying to keep some kind of order among the desperate survivors."[12]

The new nations that are caught in this struggle between the giants and that hear our exhortations about liberty, may be more aware than we are of the irony in emphasizing the threat to liberty from Communism and in almost ignoring the threat to liberty from an all-out nuclear war. When men in the West say "give me liberty or give me death" they rightly evoke a dual response. War is not likely to save liberty. And when men say this in the United States and in a few western nations, they hardly realize that they may be dooming hundreds of millions of people who never made any such choice. There is something unreal when a great western philosopher, Karl Jaspers, decides with pontifical solemnity that it is only human to prefer death to liberty. He writes: "My own thought, in view of these twin uncertainties, is that man, unlike the animals, is always free to take any risk for his freedom. If he should throw the life of mankind into the scales for liberty, he would not be taking the risk in order to die, but in order to live in freedom."[13] These are brave words but it would be well to ask a larger representation of mankind to have part in this decision since it may mean death for them before they have ever known the reality of liberty.* I think that it was A. J. Muste who coined the phrase "annihilation without representation" to indicate what is here involved.

Also, the genetic effect of the large scale use of nuclear bombs might have a destructive, if indeterminate effect, upon the quality of human life. Here the arguments about atmospheric nuclear tests are subordinate to the arguments about the effect of all-out nuclear war in which both sides poison the atmosphere with their bombs. It is sometimes said that these will affect chiefly the northern hemisphere because that is where the advanced nations live and because of the way the winds blow. But this argument only suggests a greater concentration of the poisonous effects of radiation. Also it is the northern hemisphere in which the institutions of freedom have so far flourished best. Perhaps after the advanced nations have destroyed each other, the less advanced nations a generation later will follow their example in the southern hemisphere.

As I have said, the extent of the genetic damage is indeterminate. The experts disagree about this and the policy makers are tempted to choose the experts whose calculations are most favorable to their views of policy. It seems to me that, since genetic damage is so irreversible and since it would affect the well being of so many generations, policy makers should listen to those experts who emphasize the greater danger. The revision downward of the estimates by the experts of the location of the threshold of danger in the effects of radiation has happened often enough to give us pause. A mistake at this point would be too fateful for the future of humanity to allow our generation to run serious risks.

An example of the tendency to lower the threshold of danger is a report in *The New York Times*[14] of an action of Secretary Arthur Flemming by which the government reduced by half the level of strontium 90 intake permitted human beings during a lifetime. Government scientists have often been too optimistic and slowly they

* Note Dr. Herz's comment on making this decision for future generations, p. 27.

have had to retreat. This leads me to suggest that policy makers should put the burden of proof on the more optimistic calculations.

The arguments that are advanced in this context are often appalling in their callousness and in their heedlessness about the quality of life of future generations. Herman Kahn makes a very important point of the fact that it is an advantage that the genetic damage will be spread over tens of thousands of years.[15] One can say that the full concentration of such damage within the next generation would involve so obvious a catastrophe that we could not contemplate it as the result of our actions. But we should be oppressed all the more by the prospect that ten thousand years from now children will suffer from the policy decisions which we have made or to which we have given our consent. That Herman Kahn is troubled by his own statements can be seen in the following sentences: "It is impossible to imagine a public figure stating, 'the damage due to fallout is not as serious as is sometimes implied, since most of the burden is borne by our descendants and not by our own generation.' While I believe that this statement is a defendable one, it is not one I would care to defend in the give and take of public debate."[16] Perhaps if there could be public debate on this question across the world, and if we could recognize that there is a responsibility to put the burden of proof in case of such great danger on the more optimistic experts there might be new leverage to secure agreement on nuclear disarmament. How long will it be before we see the moral incongruity in putting differences in political social systems which are temporary and which involve no biological inheritance of politically acquired characteristics ahead of irreversible genetic damage that may have its effects ten thousand years from now? And let us not dispose of this contrast by saying that the biological is merely material for biological distortions have mental and spiritual consequences.*

* The Russians have carried out a series of atmospheric nuclear tests which rightly aroused the intense moral indignation of most of humanity. So far our own country has restricted itself to underground tests and it is to be hoped that this will continue to be the case. I have been impressed by the moral confusions in common arguments used formerly by defenders of atmospheric tests in this country. We should bring these confusions to the attention of any country that employs some of the stock arguments which make light of the effects of such tests. One confusion is the comparison of the effects of tests with the effects of natural or medical radiation. The effects of natural radiation or of medical radia-

3. *My third consideration is the effect of the continued and uncontrolled arms race upon our society even if there is no large scale nuclear war.* I shall mention only three ways in which we may be dehumanized by the very process which we defend as a protection of human values.

The fear of being destroyed is bad enough but what will it do for us if for generations we live with the expectation that at any moment we may become total destroyers? I am not dogmatic about the precise moral effect of this situation. There are so many ways in which we disguise the full meaning of what we prepare to do from ourselves that there may be hidden effects on our deeper natures. Is there not a great unexplored danger to our moral sensitivities, to our habits of feeling about the meaning of life if generations are brought up with this idea that their nation is poised for a twenty-minute strike against the people of another country?

I am thinking of this not only because of the moral corruption that may come from it but also because, on a more prudential level, there may be an attrition of one of the natural sources of security for humanity. Surely the moral and human inhibition against being wholesale destroyers is one protection against wanton injury and violent death. No political system involving police power or collective security can take the place of this moral inhibition which has been strengthened by our religious traditions. During the discussion of the problem of Laos the remark was often made by journalists that the Laotians are Buddhists and because of the compassion of

---

tion may be what they are but the first is not within human control and the second may be allowed to continue if every effort is made to restrict it to what is most clearly necessary and to reduce the bad effects. The good effects of medical radiation are in a different category from the uncertain calculations concerning the good effects of atmosperic nuclear tests. A second confusion is to compare the results of nuclear tests with the number of casualties from automobile accidents. In the case of such accidents most victims choose to ride in automobiles. The moral responsibility is widely distributed among countless agents each one of whom has an expectation that there will be no fatality. This is quite different from a deliberate decision of a government in full knowledge that there will be great, if indeterminate, damage to future generations which have had no part in the decision. The third source of confusion has been the calculations of the number of persons injured in terms of percentages of all persons to be born in the next ten thousand years. These percentages may seem small but the absolute numbers may

Buddhism they have an inhibition against killing each other. This was cited as a defect that was inconvenient for our western strategy but in the long run it is a defect which is greatly needed by Christians in the West!

The many current books on power, weapons, strategy, aggression, deterrence, prudence, seem to omit one factor which is suggested by William Ernest Hocking in his recent book, *The Strength of Men and Nations*. He makes this comment about the Russians: "Whatever the mystery of Soviet motivation, however alien the Slavonic temperament and capacity for wile may be felt to be, there can be no shadow of doubt that they who share with us an official willingness to prepare weapons for the collective extinction of populations entertain not alone a fear of retaliation but an inward revulsion against their use."[17] Surely he is right. We feel this revulsion in ourselves when we allow ourselves to imagine what might happen if deterrence fails and we know that the Russian people in spite of the fact that they have been subjected to propaganda against us for the greater part of four decades are not governed by hate and are not dehumanized by their system. I know that political institutions cannot be based wholly upon this inward revulsion against being wholesale destroyers for their will always be need for police power, and where that is lacking, for some balancing of forces in society, but this moral inhibition against being destroyers is a precious resource which may be eroded by the institutions and habits and fears of the nuclear age.

The second effect of the arms race on our culture has already been discussed by other writers in this volume and reference has been made to the provocative discussion of it in the pamphlet, *Community of Fear* by Harrison Brown and James Real.[18] These authors are concerned about the effect of the arms race on the quality of our culture, on the very freedom which we are seeking to defend. We can see what is involved if the logic of civilian defence is allowed to have its way with our nation. We will construct bomb-shelters only

---

add up to a major atrocity. Also, I think that it should be said that for a government to make decisions of this kind which have direct effects on distant people who reject the decision is in itself morally questionable, and the more so when the tests are held in regions closer to those people who reject them most bitterly than to the nation that is responsible for the decision to hold them.

to find that in time they are outmoded and the source of a false sense of security. The shelters themselves will stimulate the adversary to devise ways of widening the area of lethal impact from their weapons. And so it will be necessary to construct deeper shelters and to carry on more and more of our activities underground. The logic of this leads to obvious absurdity which has been well expressed in the much quoted passage of Brown and Real:

> Once the people are convinced that they can survive the present state of the art of killing, a broad and significant new habit pattern will have been introduced and accepted, one grotesquely different from any we have known for thousands of years—that of adjusting to the idea of living in holes. From that time onward it will be simple to adjust ourselves to living in deeper holes.[19]

President Eisenhower proved to be among the prophets when in his farewell address he called attention to a third effect of the continued arms race. He spoke about the "acquisition of unwarranted influence, whether sought or unsought, by the military-industrial complex." He spoke of the danger "that public policy could itself become the captive of a scientific-technological elite."* This opens up a whole world of threats to a free and liberal society which I shall not discuss further. It is enough to note that a garrison state, ten years from now, may lose most of the values which its military power is intended to defend. I do not want to overemphasize this as a kind of bogey that should cause us to disregard the present differences between an open society and a totalitarian society but it needs to be remembered as one of the real dangers in the arms race even if there is no general war.

These considerations which I have presented do not add up to a

* Increasingly the close connection between the scientific community and, even more broadly, the academic community with defense policy adds to the complex of power which Eisenhower mentions. It was inevitable that the physical scientists would become deeply involved in defense policy in spite of the qualms of many of them and now the political scientists of the universities are coming to be deeply involved also. The link between the Rand Corporation with the air-force on the one hand and with the universities on the other dramatizes what I have in mind. Herman Kahn's book, *On Thermonuclear War,* is a great intellectual achievement and deserves much attention but it was designed by agencies within the defense department to change the attitudes of the American people about nuclear war and it was published by the press of a great university. The contribution of the academic community to government, including the defense depart-

policy. If there is great stress upon them, I can see that policy-makers will be embarrassed in fashioning any policy which includes as one element provision for nuclear deterrence. Those who struggle daily in the world of policy-making are often as aware as I am of these issues. Sometimes this awareness breaks through into solemn statements on the highest level as it did in President Kennedy's inaugural. Our government driven by this awareness is making a determined effort to break the stalemate on disarmament. This chapter in no way implies a wholesale criticism of those whose role it is to work on the level of policy within limits set both by the intransigence of Communist nations and by some patterns of public opinion in this country. But I do believe that there has been a tendency to neglect these considerations and that such neglect will prepare us for one-sided policies. In the end policy-makers may be trapped by the blindness of a nation that is governed by fear and by a concentration on the danger of Communism to freedom without adequate concern about the threat of nuclear war to humanity, to the freedom of the survivors as much as to the lives of the victims.

Discussion of moral aspects of the nuclear dilemma would remain in a vacuum if no attention is given to the realities of the cold war. In the next section of this chapter I shall make some suggestions about the presuppositions with which we may look at the cold war which to so great an extent sets the limits within which decisions about nuclear policy must be made.

III

It would have seemed enough with which to cope if we had as the one major problem the mere fact of the rapid increase of the power

---

ment, is in itself not subject to criticism. And we may welcome, first of all, the sophistication and intellectual ferment that it has brought to government. But in the long run there is a great danger that those who are most competent to criticize the policies of government will be inhibited by their responsibility in relation to those policies. There is danger that we shall confront one vast "establishment" which includes business, the military, the civilian government, the scientific community, foundations and the universities, and that informed public debate about the great moral issues connected with national defense will be inhibited. When there is so great an "establishment," one can expect the Churches to join it or to be almost silenced by it.

to destroy through the development of nuclear weapons. But added to that problem is the fact that there is a deep ideological and spiritual split in humanity which makes almost impossible the beginnings of mutual trust between the two great nuclear powers. There is no common universe of discourse and both sides assume that any agreement may be broken as soon as there is a chance for either side to win a decisive advantage over the other. As Reinhold Niebuhr has kept insisting, there is a common interest in survival which may become the minimum basis for agreements but the communication across the chasm that divides us is so faulty that even this common interest is inadequately expressed. Yet it is difficult to exaggerate the importance of one fact about the Soviet Union: its leaders now seem to be convinced that a general nuclear war would destroy a large part of their own society. When one remembers that the Marxist dialectic has no place for war except as the midwife of revolution, it is of enormous importance that Communist leaders can now look upon nuclear war as the destroyer of the fruits of revolution. The leaders of Chinese Communism do not see this so clearly, if they really see it at all. This is the source of great danger.

We on our side cannot by ourselves overcome the conflict between East and West which is the political context of our present fears of nuclear catastrophe. We can, however, make sure that our own feeling or thinking about the conflict and about the adversary is not itself controlled by ideological obsessions. There has long been a vicious circle of hostility and fear and of some real misunderstandings on both sides. I shall make some suggestions in what follows about the frame of reference from which we should look at the cold war. Again, what I say will not add up to a policy. There are and will continue to be real dangers and exasperating difficulties but a wrong frame of reference can lead us to make great mistakes in policy.

1. *It is a mistake to think of Communism as a vast undifferentiated and unchanging blot of evil to which the only response that is possible is one of undying hostility.* There are many people in this country who think of Communism in this way. If they are right, the chances of avoiding nuclear catastrophe are small indeed. But they may be wrong.

Already Communism has shown that it can differ in important

respects from country to country, as it does today as between Russia and China, as between Russia and Poland, as between Poland and Hungary. And Jugoslavia years ago proved that it is possible for a national communism to develop which seems to be no threat to its neighbors. Communism changes with the generations. It is doubtful if the changes that have taken place in the Soviet Union since the death of Stalin have been adequately grasped in this country. The fanatical revolutionary generation is passing away. The terror of the police state no longer makes Communist government a thing of horror as it was for many years under Stalin. There is ample evidence that decades of propaganda have not destroyed the humanity of the people and while generally there is intellectual rigidity, there are signs of at least quests for intellectual freedom. The Soviet system has great achievements to its credit and people in Russia can take pride in what has already been accomplished and need not put all their confidence in a future utopia. They already have a better standard of living than they have known and they expect rapid improvement under announced changes of policy.

These improvements in the Soviet Union do not mean that the Communist leaders have given up their dream of world-wide Communism. They do have much more confidence that this will be realized by peaceful means, partly because of the pull of the Russian example in the technologically underdeveloped countries. There will be no formal change of objectives but conceivably there can be real changes in priorities, in what the Russians and their leaders feel to be most important for them. The pressures of the national power of Communist nations and the pressures of Communist expansionism will create problems for us as long as we can see ahead. But war or peace may depend upon whether or not our own attitudes change to match some of the changes within the Soviet Union. The realization of the fact that Communism need not mean a hundred years of Stalinism may take away some of the desperate panic that we feel as we contemplate the successes of Communism.

There are many reasonably informed opinions about Russia. There is a good chance that the following opinion expressed by Edmund Stillman and William Pfaff in their recent much praised book is more nearly correct than the prevailing assumptions in this country. They write:

But it is safe to say that Russia today is a society only half-mad: it gives evidence of none of the transcendent madness of Nazi Germany, nor even of the unalloyed Orwellian horror of the Stalinist thirties. For Communism, whatever its defects, does not, like Nazism spring from a satanic repudiation of the rational element in man. It is a perversion of the rationalist impulse—but a perversion only. As this society is held in check, as its messianism is rebuffed, as the risk through foreign adventure is borne in, there is ground for hope that the force of reason may begin to prevail.[20]

The slogan that one would prefer to be "Red than dead" or "dead than Red" is a source of great confusion. To begin with, it is not the real alternative that we face. Many nations still have the chance to avoid both fates. As long as this is so, policy should be directed to the enabling of as many nations as possible to find a third way. Even if this choice had to be made in the sense that there could be no military resistance to the power of the Communist nations, there would remain the possibility of avoiding intellectual or spiritual acceptance of Communism, of becoming "Red." Moreover, we need not assume the unlimited power of the Communist nations to control other nations in spite of all national or local forms of resistance. Russia does not do everything that it may want to do in Poland, Finland, Jugoslavia or even Albania and these nations are all near its own borders. Its capacity to control nations at a great distance by sheer power would be more limited. Louis J. Halle has said of the Russians: "They prefer not to make a Hungary of Finland, and they would find that they could not even make a Finland of India."[21] Russia would under no circumstances find it easy to control fully the nations of western Europe that inwardly are not attracted by Communism. One of the good effects of the present plural rather than bipolar world is that both sides in the cold war have to appeal to a large body of public opinion or large bodies of public opinion in the neutral or non-committed nations. It may be that so long as a nation is organized in its own institutions for unlimited ruthlessness it will be able to pursue a policy of unlimited ruthlessness abroad but now that Russia has become less a land of domestic terror, it is likely to be more restrained in dealing with other nations. I do not contend that, if the possibility of decisive military resistance to Communist nations is abandoned, all free nations will not have bitter struggles and that some of them will not be overwhelmed by Communism, but there will be degrees of Communist control or influence, for Communist power is not invincible regardless of geography and regardless of the internal health of a country.

2. We need to take more seriously than we do the fact that the cold war is not primarily a military conflict.

The nuclear arms race and the threat of possible nuclear destruction are bad enough but think how much worse these would be if we knew it to be a fact that the Soviet Union was bent on extending Communism primarily by means of military aggression? The fact that the cold war came so recently after the conflict with Nazism made it natural for us to carry over into this situation feelings and assumptions which were justified in the context of the earlier struggle. For Nazism military aggression was the primary instrument, and propaganda and infiltration were quite secondary. After all, Nazism had little to offer to anyone except Nordic white men and, apart from some illusions that flourished on German soil, what it offered them could soon be identified as poison. For Communism the chief instrument of advance is the Communist idea, reinforced by the achievements of Russia and by the strength of revolutionary parties and the wiles of conspirators, and military power is auxiliary.

George Kennan has often emphasized the incongruity of our interpreting the cold war primarily in military terms. In his recent book, *Russia and the West under Lenin and Stalin,* he is very clear on this point. If what he says were really believed in this country, there would be no immediate lessening of our responsibility to maintain a military balance in the world but again some of the panic would go out of our attitude. In speaking about the possibility of a "single grand military conflict" he says:

> I cannot think of a time when the Soviet government desired that there be such a conflict, planned to launch it, or staked its hopes and expectations for the victory of world socialism on the effects of such an encounter. Central to the Soviet view of how socialism was to triumph on a world scale has always been the operation of social and political forces within the capitalist countries; and, while Moscow has always recognized that civil violence would have a legitimate place in the operation of these processes—while it has not hesitated in certain instances to promote or even to organize such civil

violence; while it has even considered, in fact, that the use of the Soviet armies in a subsidiary capacity might be justified at one point or another as a means of hastening or completing an otherwise inevitable process—it has never regarded action by its own forces as the *main* agency for the spread of world revolution. It has not, in other words, sought to obtain its objectives by the traditional processes of open and outright warfare. In the course of the last twenty years, I have labored many hours to explain to other Americans the nature of the Soviet threat as I saw it; in no respect have I found it so difficult to obtain understanding as in the presentation of this one simple fact.[22]

Perhaps the chief obstacle to such understanding is the tendency in this country to assume that, because Communism and Nazism are both totalitarian, they must pose the same kind of threat to the free world. The Communist strategy, with its subsidiary use of military threats and of military force, may be more difficult to resist than Nazism. In some ways its dynamism is a greater danger in the sense that its appeal is greater. But the changes in the Soviet Union may lead us to judge that it is in the long term not as absolutely destructive of all values as Nazism was with its gas chambers and we should be able to oppose it by means which are constructive. Indeed if Communism wakes us up to the need of social revolution in half of the world and causes us to stretch ourselves to help people to find constructive alternatives, it will have to that extent served a useful purpose. Can anything be more obvious than this simple fact: that the nations which are today most vulnerable to Communist influence are nations whose problems cannot be solved by the use of any kind of weapons. The more independent nations there are that have both reasonably stable and effective governments and that deal hopefully with their economic and social problems, the less will be the power of Communism in the world. Instead of causing us fear, the prospect of having a part in such developments should be a source of national exhilaration. If this is not so, the cause of our failures will not be the wickedness or the nuclear power of the Communists but our own inability as a rich and conservative nation to understand the needs and the temper of the nations which Communists have their best chance to win.

3. *We should distinguish more explicitly than is usually the case between our attitude toward Communism as an established reality in the Soviet Union and in China and our attitude toward the extension of Communism by force or intimidation by the Soviet Union or China to other lands.*

There is no intention among those responsible for policy in the United States to seek to destroy Communism in the Soviet Union. But there is a habit of such deep hostility to Communism there and everywhere that it is not strange that leaders of the Soviet Union feel that we are their mortal enemies. This relationship of mortal enmity greatly enhances the danger that nuclear weapons will finally be used. When Walter Lippmann was in Moscow in 1958 he was convinced that Khrushchev really believed that if the United States "finds that it is going to lose the cold war, it is likely to resort to hot war."[23] Lippmann goes on to say: "That is not what he said, but I came to think that it was what he meant after an interesting passage in which he talked about the American fear and hatred of Communism." It is significant that Lippmann associated this attitude with Khrushchev's recognition of our fear and hatred. Even if this interpretation by Lippmann is exaggerated a bit, if there is any substantial truth in it, the reassurance of the Russians on this point should be high on our agenda. But this will be difficult because communication across the chasm is so poor. Can we not find ways of demonstrating our acceptance of Communism as a reality in Russia that has come to stay, that can be expected to change but which we should not attempt to displace? If this were dramatized we could continue to make clear our resolve to do what we can to prevent the extension of Communism by force or intimidation, and to help nations which are now vulnerable to Communism to find alternatives to it which are compatible with some forms of openness and freedom in society. We need not insist on our own forms of freedom but we should help any nation that has a will of its own to remain independent to do so.

When I first mentioned this distinction between our attitude toward nations in which Communism is established, I referred to China as well as Russia. China does create a more difficult problem. It is in the early stages of revolutionary fanaticism. It may not fully realize the threat of a nuclear war to its own life. And yet I am suggesting that we should no longer act as though our nation were still a participant in the Chinese civil war. Symbolically we seem to be so because of our alliance with the Nationalist government. Here a distinction must be made more explicitly between a commitment to preserve the freedom of Taiwan and partnership with the Nationalist government in the continuing Chinese civil war. What hope there is for the people of China lies probably in developments within Communism in China rather than in the displacement of Communism. In any case the United States must recognize the limits of its powers and it must not take responsibility for seeking to displace the Communist regime in that country. If it is assumed that we are still merely biding our time until we can give effective support to a counter-revolution in China, again the danger of nuclear war will be very great.

The phrase "victory in the cold war" is sometimes used by those who have exaggerated notions of American power, who seem to assume that our nation is commissioned to control the main currents of human history, and who neglect the danger of nuclear war. The distinction which I have made between our acceptance of Communism as a reality in Russia and China and our acceptance of the responsibility to help nations which seek to remain free from the imposition of Communism to do so suggests the sound alternative to the idea of victory in the cold war. As long as that idea of victory appears to be our goal, we must expect Russia and China to fear us just as we fear them. I do not believe that anything that we say will dispel this fear. But in the course of years a change of attitude on our part may come to be expressed in such a way as to reduce this fear of attack by us. In working to achieve this result the United States will increase the chances that nuclear weapons may not be used.

*

The persons who are responsible for American policy at the present time are in a position of the greatest difficulty. They are right in believing that this nation does have a responsibility to preserve strength that will balance the power of the Communist world to an extent that is sufficient to preserve opportunities for nations which are not already under Communist domination to choose their own social system and their own form of government. We do not have to choose between a world dominated by Communism and a world destroyed by war and our government has the extraordinarily difficult task of seeking to prevent both of these evil conditions. The military factor in fulfilling this task is necessary though by itself it cannot solve any of the internal problems that make nations vulnerable to Communist penetration. If we become obsessed with this military factor we will do the wrong things. If we let down our guard, we may create conditions which will cause many nations to surrender to Communist pressure and so narrow the area of freedom that free nations will lose confidence in themselves. At some stage our own nation might become so isolated that it would take on a fatal obsession with military power and perhaps in a state of panic precipitate the war that is most feared. If there is the hope in creative developments within the Communist world which I have described, we may well be guided by this hope while we do what is necessary now to prevent the extension of Communist power and help the nations with political and moral strength to develop institutions which are for them viable alternatives to Communism. If we can keep the world from domination by any one system long enough, we may hope that interaction between the mature institutions of both the Communist world and the "free world" will be good for both worlds.

In the meantime, we do not see such a hopeful future with any clarity. We must make our decisions in the light of many immediate threats. We cannot trust in a posture of deterrence by itself to keep the peace for long. The achievement of control of nuclear weapons on the way to disarmament is essential if there is to be peace or if mankind is to be spared the dehumanizing effects of an endless arms race. The ethical issues raised in this chapter about nuclear war and about the arms race are not the only issues by which either policy-makers or the public should be guided. But if they are neglected we are likely to develop a myopia governed by fear and hostility and by a false confidence in what military power can accomplish; and we are likely to choose policies which so lack balance that we and our adversaries will stumble into nuclear catastrophe.

NOTES

1. Princeton University Press, 1960.
2. *Commentary*, October, 1961, p. 281.
3. *On Thermonuclear War*, p. 91.
4. *Ibid.*, p. 91.

5. *Ibid.*, p. 275.

6. *Worldview*, April, 1961.

7. Commission on "The Relation of the Church to the War in the Light of the Christian Faith." Report in *Social Action*, December 15, 1944.

8. Harper and Brothers, 1960, p. 28.

9. Quoted in *Worldview*, February, 1961.

10. *Christianity and Crisis*, November 13, 1961.

11. *International Conflict in the Twentieth Century*, Harper and Brothers, 1960, p. 95.

12. *The New York Herald Tribune*, September 14, 1961.

13. *The Future of Mankind*, University of Chicago Press, 1961, p. 168.

14. February 26, 1960.

15. *On Thermonuclear War*, p. 48.

16. *Ibid.*, p. 49.

17. Harper and Brothers, 1959, p. 188.

18. Published by the Fund for the Republic, 1960.

19. *Ibid.*, pp. 38-39.

20. *The New Politics: America and the End of the Postwar World.* Coward McCann, 1961, p. 85.

21. *The New Republic*, February 29, 1960.

22. Atlantic-Little Brown, 1961, p. 389.

23. *The New York Herald Tribune*, November 11, 1958.

Explorations into the
unilateral disarmament position

BY ERICH FROMM

ERICH FROMM *is Chairman of the Department of Psychoanalysis of the Medical School at the National University of Mexico. After studying psychology, sociology and philosophy at various German universities, he graduated (1931) from the Berlin Institute of Psychoanalysis. Since then he has held positions with the New School for Social Research, the William Alanson White Institute of Psychiatry, Psychoanalysis and Psychology, and Michigan State University. Among his numerous publications are* Man for Himself, Escape from Freedom, Psychoanalysis and Religion, The Sane Society, The Art of Loving, *and* May Man Prevail?

Dr. Fromm is a sponsor of the National Committee for a Sane Nuclear Policy, which favors cessation of atomic testing and universal controlled disarmament, and is active in the Committees of Correspondence, which also stands for universal nuclear disarmament and for the solution of all foreign policy problems by negotiation.

THE term "unilateral" in relation to disarmament has been used in two different meanings. First, and more frequently, in the sense of the unilateral and unconditional dismantling of a country's military establishment. Secondly, by Charles Osgood, in the sense of "graduated unilateral action" toward multilateral disarmament. Since unilateral disarmament in the first sense of the term will hardly be acceptable to the United States or the Soviet Union under existing conditions, this essay proposes, as a practical step, the second and limited concept of graduated unilateral action, which might also be called *unilateral initiative in taking practical steps towards disarmament.* The basic idea underlying this concept is that of a radical change of our method of negotiating multilateral disarmament. This change implies that we give up the present method of bargaining in which every concession we make is dependent on a corresponding and guaranteed concession on the part of the Russians; that, instead, we take, unilaterally, gradual steps toward disarmament in the expectation that the Russians will reciprocate and that, thus, the present deadlock in the negotiations for universal disarmament can be broken through.

In order to describe the nature of this policy of unilateral steps, I cannot improve on the following description by Osgood, who, as far as I know, was the first one to express this idea in two brilliant and profound articles.[1] "To be maximally effective," he writes, "in inducing the enemy to reciprocate, a unilateral act (1) should, in terms of *military aggression,* be clearly disadvantageous to the side making it, yet not cripplingly so; (2) should be such as to be clearly perceived by the enemy as reducing his external threat; (3) should not increase the enemy's threat to our heartland;* (4) should be such that reciprocal action by the enemy is clearly available and clearly indicated; (5) should be announced in advance and widely publicized to ally, neutral and

* This condition is in my opinion to be taken only as an optimal *desideratum,* since any weakening of one power's aggressive potential means strategically some increase in the opponent's aggressive potential.

enemy countries—as regards the nature of the act, its purpose as part of a consistent policy, and the expected reciprocation; but (6) should not demand prior commitment to reciprocation by the enemy as a condition for its commission."[2]

As to the specific steps which should be taken in this fashion, it would require a great deal of further thought, aided by competent specialists. But in order to give at least an idea of the concrete steps this policy would envisage, I want to mention the following (some of them in agreement with Osgood): sharing of scientific information; stopping of atomic tests; troop reductions; evacuation of one or more military bases; discontinuation of German rearmament; etc. The expectation is that the Russians are as willing as we are to avoid war, hence that they will begin to reciprocate and that once the course of mutual suspicion has been reversed, bigger steps can be taken which may lead to complete bilateral disarmament. Futhermore, I believe that disarmament negotiations should be paralleled by *political* negotiations, which aim essentially at mutual noninterference on the basis of the recognition of the *status quo*.[3] Here, too (and again in essential agreement with Osgood's position), unilateral steps such as the recognition of the Oder-Neisse line and admission of China to the United Nations would be taken in the expectation of reciprocation by the Russians (i.e., curbing of Chinese aggression, noninterference in the Middle and Far East).

What are the premises underlying the proposition for unilateral steps towards disarmament? (At this point I shall mention only some fundamental ones, while others will be discussed in the second part of this essay which presents the argument for total unilateral disarmament.) They are briefly: (1) that, as indicated before, the present method of negotiations does not seem to lead to the goal of bilateral disarmament because of the deeply ingrained mutual suspicions and fears; (2) that without achieving *complete* disarmament, the armament race will continue and lead to the destruction of our civilization as well as that of the Russians or, even without the outbreak of a war, will slowly undermine and eventually destroy the values in defense of which we are risking our physical existence; (3) that while unilateral steps constitute a definite risk (and must do so by the very nature of the idea), the risk at every step is not a crippling one and is infinitely smaller than the danger we run by the continuation of the arms race.

Even though the broader concept of complete—rather than graduated—unilateral disarmament is, as stated before, not a practical possibility in the near future, as far as the United States and the USSR are concerned, I believe it worthwhile to present the arguments for this position for the following reasons: thinking through the arguments for a radical—even though practically unacceptable position—contributes to breaking through the thought barrier which prevents us now from getting out of the dangerous circle of seeking peace by means of threat and counterthreat. Taking seriously the reasoning which supports the unpopular position of complete unilateral disarmament can open up new approaches and viewpoints which are important even if our practical aim is that of "graduated unilateral action" or even only that of negotiated bilateral disarmament. I believe that the difficulty of arriving at complete disarmament lies to a large extent in the frozen stereotypes of feelings and thought habits on both sides and that any attempt at unfreezing these patterns and of rethinking the whole problem can be of importance in finding a way out of the present dangerous impasse.

The proposal for complete unilateral disarmament has been advocated from a religious, moral or pacifist position by such men as Victor Gollancz, Lewis Mumford, and some Quakers. It has also been supported by men like Bertrand Russell, Stephen King-Hall, and others, who are not opposed to the use of force under all or any circumstances, yet who are uncompromisingly opposed both to thermonuclear war and to all and any preparation for it. This writer finds himself somewhat between the position of the strict pacifists and men like Bertrand Russell and Stephen King-Hall.[4]

The difference between these two groups, however, is not as fundamental as it may seem. They are united by their critical attitude toward the irrational aspects of international politics and by their deep reverence for life. They share the conviction of the oneness of the human race and faith in the spiritual and intellectual potentialities of man. They follow the dictates of their conscience in refusing to have any "part in making millions of women and children and noncombatants hostages for the behavior of their own governments."[5] Whether they think in theistic terms or in those of nontheistic humanism (in the sense of the philosophic continuum from Stoic to eighteenth-century Enlightenment philosophy), they all are rooted in the same spiritual tradition and are unwilling to compromise with its principles. They are united by their uncompromising opposition to any kind of idolatry, including the idolatry of the state. While their opposition to the Soviet system is rooted precisely in this attitude against idolatry, they are critical of idolatry whenever it appears in the Western world whether it is in the name of God or of democracy.

While there is no proponent of unilateral disarmament who does not believe that the individual must be willing to give his life for the sake of his supreme values, if such an ultimate necessity arises, they are all equally convinced that to risk the life of the human race, or even the results of its best efforts in the last five thousand years, is immoral and irresponsible. As warfare becomes at once more sense-less and more devastating, the convergence between religious pacifist, humanist, and pragmatic opponents to nuclear armament grows.

From the standpoint of the proponents of unilateral disarmament, to continue the armament race is catastrophic, *whether the deterrent works or not*. In the first place, they have little faith that the deter-rent will prevent the outbreak of a thermonuclear war.* They be-lieve that the results of a thermonuclear war would be such that in the very "best" case they completely belie the idea that we ought to fight such a war in order to save our democratic way of life. There is no need to enter the guessing game as to whether one-third or two-thirds of the population of the two opponents and what pro-portion of the neutral world (depending on how the wind blows) will be destroyed. This is a guessing game that verges on madness;

---

* This premise is shared by the report of the National Planning Association of America: *1970 Without Arms Control; Implications of Modern Weapons Tech-nology* (by NPA Special Project Committee on Security through Arms Control; Planning Pamphlet no. 104, May 1958, Washington, D.C.), which states: "Not only does the danger of war remain a possibility, but the probability totalled over time increases, becoming a certainty if sufficient time elapses without succeeding in finding alternatives." Or, E. Finley Carter, President of the Stanford Research Institute, writes: "In the search for security through the application of technology to weapons for destruction, the Soviet block and the Western allies have created a mortal common enemy—the threat of accidental nuclear war" (*SRI Journal*, Stan-ford Research Institute, Fourth Quarter, 1959, vol. 3, p. 198). Herman Kahn also concludes, "It is most unlikely that the world can live with an uncontrolled arms race lasting for several decades" (*ibid.*, p. 139). He emphasizes that it is unrealistic to believe that war has become impossible because of its extremely destructive character.

The advisor on Science and Technology of the Democratic Advisory Council for to consider the possibility of the destruction of 30%, 60%, or 90% of one's own and the enemy's population as an acceptable (although, of course, most undesirable) result of one's policy is indeed approaching pathology. The increasing split between intellect and affect, which is so characteristic of our Western development in the last centuries, has reached its dangerous, schizoid peak in the calm and allegedly rational way in which we can discuss possible world destruction as a result of our own action. It does not take much imagination to visualize that sudden destruction and the threat of slow death to a large part of the American population, or the Russian population, or large parts of the world, will create such a panic, fury, and despair as could only be compared with the mass psychosis resulting from the Black Death in the Middle Ages. The traumatic effects of such a catastrophe would lead to a new form of primitive barbarism, to the resurgence of the most archaic elements, which are still potentialities in every man and of which we have had ample evidence in the terror systems of Hitler and Stalin. It would sound most unlikely to many students of human nature and psychopathology that human beings could cherish freedom, respect for life or love after having witnessed and participated in the unlimited cruelty of man against man which thermonuclear war would mean. It is a psychological fact that acts of brutality have a brutalizing effect on the participants and lead to more brutality.

BUT WHAT IF THE DETERRENT WORKS?

What is the likely future of the social character of man in an armed world, where, no matter how complex the problems or how full the satisfactions of any particular society, the biggest and most pervasive

---

of 27 December, 1959, declared: "All-out nuclear war seems not only possible but probable as long as we pursue our present military policies and fail to achieve international agreements of broad scope designed to alleviate this unstable situation. The triggering of a nuclear war by mistake, by misadventure or by miscalculation is a constant danger." It must be stressed that the danger lies not only in technical errors, but equally in the blundering decision-making by political and military leaders. If one remembers the political and military blunders committed by many of the leaders in the conduct of the wars of 1914 and 1939, it is not difficult to visualize that, given present-day weapons, the same type of leaders will blow the world to pieces, in spite of good intentions.

reality in any man's life is the poised missile, the humming data processor connected to it, the waiting radiation counters and seismographs, the over-all technocratic perfection (overlying the nagging but impotent fear of its imperfection) of the mechanism of holocaust? To live for any length of time under the constant threat of destruction creates certain psychological effects in most human beings—fright, hostility, callousness, a hardening of the heart, and a resulting indifference to all the values we cherish. Such conditions will transform us into barbarians—though barbarians equipped with the most complicated machines. If we are serious in claiming that our aim is to preserve freedom (that is, to prevent the subordination of the individual under an all-powerful state), we must admit that this freedom will be lost, whether the deterrent works or does not work.

Aside from these psychological facts, the continuation of the arms race constitutes a particular threat to Western culture. In the process of conquering nature, producing and consuming have become Western man's main preoccupation—the goal of his life. We have transformed means into ends. We manufacture machines which are like men, and we produce men who are like machines. In his work, the individual is managed as a part of a production team. During his leisure time, he is manipulated as a consumer who likes what he is told to like and yet has the illusion that he follows his own taste. In centering his life around the production of things, man himself is in danger of becoming a thing, worshiping the idols of the production machine and the state while he is under the illusion of worshiping God. "Things are in the saddle and ride mankind," as Emerson has put it. Circumstances which we created have consolidated themselves into powers which rule over us. The technical and bureaucratic system we have built tells us what to do, it decides for us. We may not be in danger of becoming slaves, but we are in danger of becoming robots, and the human values of our tradition are threatened—integrity, individuality, responsibility, reason, and love. Talking about these values more and more becomes an empty ritual.[6]

This trend toward a world of impotent men directed by virile machines (both in the United States and in the Soviet Union)— brought about by technological and demographic factors, and by the increasing centralization and bureaucracy in big corporations and government—will reach the point of no return if we continue the arms race. Dangerous as our present situation is, we still have a chance to put man back into the saddle, to effect a renaissance of the spiritual values of the great humanistic tradition. Unless such a renaissance occurs, unless we can achieve a radical revitalization of the spirit on which our culture is founded, we shall lose the vitality necessary for survival and we shall decay, just as many other great powers have decayed in history. The real threat to our existence is not Communist ideology, it is not even the Communist military power —it is the hollowness of our beliefs, the fact that freedom, individuality, and faith have become empty formulas, that God has become an idol, that our vitality is sapped because we have no vision except that of having more of the same. It seems that a great deal of the hatred of Communism is, in the last analysis, based on a deep disbelief in the spiritual values of democracy. Hence, instead of experiencing love of what we are *for,* we experience hate of what we are *against.* If we continue to live in fear of extinction and to plan mass destruction of others, the last chance for a revival of our humanist-spiritual tradition will be lost.

BENEFITS AND DANGERS OF UNILATERAL DISARMAMENT

If these are the dangers of the policy of the deterrent, what do the proponents of unilateral disarmament consider to be the benefits—and the dangers—of their policy?

The most likely result of unilateral disarmament—whether it be undertaken by the United States or by the Soviet Union—is that it would prevent war. The main reason which could impel either the Soviet Union or the United States to atomic war is the constant fear of being attacked and pulverized by the opponent. This position is succinctly expressed by Herman Kahn, who is in no way a proponent of unilateral disarmament. Kahn states that, "aside from the ideological differences and the problem of security itself, there does not seem to be any objective quarrel between the United States and Russia that justifies the risks and costs that we subject each other to. The big thing that the Soviet Union and the United States have to fear from each other is fear itself."[7] If, indeed, the main cause of war lies in mutual fear, then the disarmament of either the Soviet Union or the United States would most likely do away with this major cause and, thus, with the probability of war.

But are there motives other than fear which could prompt the Soviet Union to try for world conquest? One such motive could be economic interest in expansion, which was a basic motivation for the initiation of war in the nineteenth century and also for the first two World Wars. Exactly here we see the difference between the nature of the conflicts in 1914 or 1939 and the present situation. In World War I, Germany threatened British markets and the French sources of coal and iron; in 1939, Hitler needed territorial conquest for the economic expansion he wanted. Today, neither the Soviet Union nor the United States has overriding economic interests in the conquest of markets and supplies, since a 2 or 3 percent rise in the level of national productivity would bring a greater advantage than would any military conquest, and, moreover, since each has the capital, raw material, supplies, and population for a constant increase in its general productivity.*

The more serious possible motive is found in the fear, widely held in the United States, that the Soviet Union is out to conquer the world for Communism and that, if the United States disarmed, Russia would be all the more eager to achieve her wish for world domination. This idea of Russian intentions is based on an erroneous appreciation of the nature of the present-day Soviet Union. It is true that under Lenin and Trotzky the Russian Revolution was aimed at conquering the capitalistic world (or at least, Europe) for Communism, partly because the Communist leaders were convinced that there was no possibility of success for Communist Russia unless the highly industrialized states of Europe (or at least Germany) joined their system, and partly because they were prompted by the belief that the victory of the Communist revolution in the world would bring about the fulfillment of their secular-messianic hopes.

The failure of these hopes and the ensuing victory of Stalin

---

* For the very same reasons, there is a real chance for the future abolition of war, a chance which never existed in the past. In most of man's history, the improvement of his material situation required an increase in human energy (slaves), additional land for cattle raising or agriculture, or new sources of raw materials. The techniques of the present and of the future will permit an increase in material wealth by an increased industrial and—indirectly—an agricultural productivity, without the need of enslaving or robbing others. At present and in the future, war would have as its only "rationale" the irrationality of human desire for power and conquest.

brought about a complete change in the nature of Soviet Communism. The annihiliation of almost all the old Bolsheviks was only a symbolic act for the destruction of the old revolutionary idea. Stalin's slogan of "socialism in one country" covered one simple aim— the rapid industrialization of Russia, which the Czarist system had not accomplished. Russia repeated the same process of accumulating capital which Western capitalism had gone through in the eighteenth and nineteenth centuries. The essential difference is that, while in these centuries in the West the sanctions were purely economic, the Stalinist system now developed political sanctions of direct terror; in addition, it employed socialist ideology to sugar-coat the exploitation of the masses. The Stalinist system was neither a socialist nor a revolutionary system, but a state-managerialism based on ruthless methods of planning and economic centralization.

The period of Khrushchevism is characterized by the fact that capital accumulation has succeeded to a point where the population can enjoy a great deal more consumption and is less forced to make sacrifices; as a result, the political terror can be greatly reduced.

But Khrushchevism has by no means changed the basic character of Soviet society in one essential respect: it is not a revolutionary nor a socialist regime, but one of the most conservative, class-ridden regimes anywhere in the Western world, humanly coercive, economically effective. While the aim of democratic socialism was the emancipation of man, the overcoming of his alienation, and the eventual abolition of the state, the "socialist" slogans used in Soviet Russia reflect empty ideologies, and the social reality is the very opposite of true socialism. The ruling class of the Soviet Union is no more revolutionary than the Renaissance popes were followers of the teachings of Christ. To try to explain Khrushchev by quoting Marx, Lenin, or Trotzky shows an utter failure to understand this historical development which has taken place in the Soviet Union and an incapacity to appreciate the difference between facts and ideologies. It should be added that our attitude is the best propaganda service the Russians could wish for. Against the facts, they try to convince the workers of Western Europe and the peasants in Asia that they represent the ideas of socialism, of a classless society, etc. The Western attitude, of falling for this propaganda, does exactly what the Russians want: to confirm these claims. (Unfortunately very few people except democratic socialists have sufficient knowledge of the difference between socialism and its distorted and corrupt form which calls itself Soviet socialism.) In fact, it seems that within the Soviet Union, Communist ideology has worn as thin as religion has in the West and that the only ones who take Communist ideology seriously are the people in the Western world—not the average Russian.

The role of Russia is still more complicated by the fact that Russia feels threatened by a potentially expansionist China. Russia one day might be in the same position with regard to China as we believe we are in relation to Russia. If the threat to Russia from the United States were to disappear, Russia could devote her energy to coping with the threat from China, unless by universal disarmament this threat would cease to exist.

The above-mentioned considerations indicate that the dangers which might arise if the Soviet Union were not to give up its armaments are more remote than they seem to many. Would the Soviet Union use her military superiority to try to occupy the United States or Western Europe? Aside from the fact it would be exceedingly difficult, to say the least, for the Soviet Union's agents to run the economic and political machines of the United States or Western Europe, and aside from the fact that there is no vital need for Russia to conquer these territories, it would be most inconvenient to try to do so—and for a reason which is generally not sufficiently appreciated. Even the pro-Communist workers in Western Europe have no idea of the degree of coercion to which they would have to submit under a Soviet system. They, as well as non-Communist workers, would oppose the new authorities, who would be forced to use tanks and machine guns against the protesting workers. This would encourage revolutionary tendencies in the satellite states, or even within the Soviet Union, and be most undesirable to the Soviet rulers; it would especially endanger Khrushchev's policy of liberalization, and hence his whole political position.

Eventually the Soviet Union might try to exploit its military superiority for the penetration of Asia and Africa. This is possible, but, with our present policy of the deterrent, it is doubtful whether the United States would really be willing to start a thermonuclear war in order to prevent the Russians from gaining certain advantages in the world outside of Europe and the Americas.

All these assumptions may be wrong. The position of the proponents of unilateral disarmament is that the chance that they are wrong is much smaller than the chance that the continuation of the arms race will finish civilization as we cherish it.

SOME PSYCHOLOGICAL CONSIDERATIONS

One cannot discuss the question of what might happen as a result of unilateral disarmament—or, for that matter, of any mutual disarmament—without examining some psychological arguments. The most popular one is that "the Russians cannot be trusted." If "trust" is meant in a moral sense, it is unfortunately true that political leaders can rarely be trusted. The reason lies in the split between private and public morals: the state, having become an idol, justifies any immorality if committed in its interest, while the very same political leaders would not commit the same acts if they were acting in behalf of their own private interests. However, there is another meaning to "trust in people," a meaning which is much more relevant to the problem of politics: the trust that they are sane and rational beings, and that they will act accordingly. If I deal with an opponent in whose sanity I trust, I can appreciate his motivations and to some extent predict them, because there are certain rules and aims, like that of survival or that of commensurateness between aims and means, which are common to all sane people. Hitler could not be trusted because he was lacking in sanity, and this very lack destroyed both him and his regime. It seems quite clear that the Russian leaders of today are sane and rational people; therefore, it is important not only to know what they are capable of, but also to predict what they might be motivated to do.*

* Whether or not political leaders are sane is not a matter of historical accident. Any government which has set out to do the impossible—for instance, to achieve equality and justice when the requisite material conditions are lacking—will produce fanatical and irrational leaders. This was the case with Robespierre, as it was with Stalin. Or, a government which tries to reconcile the interests of the most backward social class (the lower middle class) with those of the economically progressive classes (workers and businessmen) as the Nazi government did, again will produce fanatical and irrational leaders. The Soviet Union today is on the road toward solving its economic problems successfully; hence it is not surprising that her leaders are realistic men of common sense.

This question of the leaders' and the people's sanity leads to another consideration which affects us as much as it does the Russians. In the current discussion of armament control, many arguments are based on the question of what is *possible,* rather than on what is *probable.* The difference between these two modes of thinking is precisely the difference between *paranoid* and *sane* thinking. The paranoiac's unshakable conviction in the validity of his delusion rests upon the fact that it is logically possible, and, so, unassailable. It is logically possible that his wife, children, and colleagues hate him and are conspiring to kill him. The patient cannot be convinced that his delusion is *impossible;* he can only be told that it is exceedingly *unlikely.* While the latter position requires an examination and evaluation of the facts and also a certain amount of faith in life, the paranoid position can satisfy itself with the possibility alone. I submit that our political thinking suffers from such paranoid trends. We should be concerned, not with the possibilities, but rather with the probabilities and that means we should examine the political realities soberly, objectively and thoroughly. This is the only sane and realistic way of conducting the affairs of national as well as of individual life.

Again on the psychological plane, there are certain misunderstandings of the radical disarmament position which occur in many of the discussions. First of all, the position of unilateral disarmament has been understood as one of submission and resignation. On the contrary, the pacifists as well as the humanist pragmatists believe that unilateral disarmament is possible only as an expression of a deep spiritual and moral change within ourselves: it is an act of courage and resistance—not one of cowardice or surrender. Forms of resistance differ in accordance with the respective viewpoints. On the other hand, Gandhists and men like King-Hall advocate nonviolent resistance, which undoubtedly requires the maximum of courage and faith; they refer to the example of Indian resistance against Britain or Norwegian resistance against the Nazis. This point of view is succinctly expressed in *Speak Truth to Power* (see Note 4):

> Thus, we dissociate ourselves from the basically selfish attitude that has been miscalled pacifism, but that might be more accurately described as a kind of irresponsible antimilitarism. We dissociate ourselves also from utopianism. Though the choice of nonviolence

involves a radical change in men, it does not require perfection. . . . We have tried to make it clear that readiness to accept suffering— rather than inflict it on others—is the essence of the nonviolent life, and that we must be prepared if called upon to pay the ultimate price. Obviously, if men are willing to spend billions of treasure and countless lives in war, they cannot dismiss the case for nonviolence by saying that in a nonviolent struggle people might be killed! It is equally clear that where commitment and the readiness to sacrifice are lacking, nonviolent resistance cannot be effective. On the contrary, it demands greater discipline, more arduous training, and more courage than its violent counterpart.[8]

Some think of armed resistance, of men and women defending their lives and their freedom with rifles, pistols, or knives. It is not unrealistic to think that both forms of resistance, nonviolent or violent, might deter an aggressor from attacking. At least, it is more realistic than to think that the use of thermonuclear weapons could lead to a victory for democracy.

The proponents of "security by armament" sometimes accuse their opponents of having an unrealistic, flatly optimistic picture of the nature of man. They remind us that this "perverse human being has a dark, illogical, irrational side."[9] They even go so far as to say that "the paradox of nuclear deterrence is a variant of the fundamental Christian paradox. In order to *live,* we must express our willingness *to kill* and to die."[10] Apart from this crude falsification of Christian teaching, we are by no means oblivious of the potential evil within man and of the tragic aspect of life. But, there is no tragedy in irresponsibility and carelessness: there is no meaning or dignity in the idea of the destruction of mankind and of civilization. Man has in himself a potential for evil; his whole existence is beset by dichotomies rooted in the very conditions of his existence. But these truly tragic aspects must not be confused with the results of stupidity and lack of imagination, with the willingness to stake the future of mankind on a gamble.

Furthermore, it is true that an individual's decision to give his life for the sake of a fellowman's life, or of his integrity, and his convictions, is one of the greatest moral achievements man is capable of. But it is a *moral* achievement only if it is the result of an *individual's decision,* a decision not motivated by vanity, depression, masochism, but by devotion to another person's life, or to an idea. Few people have the courage and conviction to make this supreme sacrifice for the sake of an idea. The majority are not even willing to risk a job for the sake of their convictions. But if this decision is made not individually but nationally, it loses its ethical significance. It is not an authentic decision which is made by a person, but a decision made *for* millions by a few leaders who, in order to get the individuals to accept the "ethical" decisions, have to make them drunk with passions of hate and fear.

Finally, to take up one last criticism, directed against the position of unilateral disarmament: that it is "soft" on Communism. The unilateral position is precisely based on the negation of the Soviet principle of the omnipotence of the state. Just because the spokesmen for unilateral disarmament are drastically opposed to the supremacy of the state, they do not want to grant the state the ever-increasing power which is unavoidable in the arms race, and they deny the right of the state to make decisions which can lead to the destruction of a great part of humanity and can doom future generations. If the basic conflict between the Soviet system and the democratic world is the question of the defense of the individual against the encroachment of an omnipotent state, then, indeed, the position for unilateral disarmament is the one which is most radically opposed to the Soviet principle.

After having discussed the arguments for unilateral disarmament (in the broad sense), I want to return to the practical proposition of unilateral steps toward disarmament. I do not deny that there are risks involved in this limited form of unilateral action but considering the fact that the present method of negotiations has produced no results and that the chances that they will in the future are rather slim, considering furthermore the grave risk involved in the continuation of the arms race, I believe that it is practically and morally justified to take this risk. At present we are caught in a position with little chance for survival, unless we want to take refuge in hopes. *If* we have enought shelters, *if* there is enough time for a warning and strategic evacuation of cities, *if* the "United States' active offenses and active defenses can gain control of the military situation after only a few exchanges,"[11] we might have only five, or twenty-five, or seventy million killed. However, if these conditions do not materialize, "an enemy could, by repeated strikes, reach almost any level of death and destruction he wished."[12] (And, I assume, the same threat exists for the Soviet Union.) In such a situation, when war can be unleashed by fanatics, lunatics or men of ambition, it is imperative to shake off the inertia of our accustomed thinking, to seek for new approaches to the problem, and above all, to see new alternatives to the present choices that confront us.

NOTES

1. Charles E. Osgood's "Suggestions for Winning the Real War with Communism," "Conflict Resolution," vol. III, no. 4, December 1959, p. 131, and also "A Case for Graduated Unilateral Disarmament," *Bulletin of Atomic Scientists,* vol. XVI, no. 4, pp. 127 ff.
2. Charles E. Osgood's "Suggestions for Winning the Real War with Communism," p. 316.
3. Cf. my discussion of the political problems in *May Man Prevail? An Inquiry into the Facts and Fictions of Foreign Policy.* A Doubleday Anchor Book.
4. Bertrand Russell, *Common Sense and Nuclear Warfare.* London: G. Allen & Unwin, Ltd., 1959. Stephen King-Hall, *Defense in the Nuclear Age.* Nyack, N.Y.: Fellowship Publications, 1959. Jerome Davis and General H. B. Hester, *On the Brink.* New York: Lyle Stuart, 1959. Lewis Mumford, *The Human Way Out.* Pendell Hill Pamphlet no. 97, 1958. C. W. Mills, *The Causes of World War Three.* New York, 1959. George F. Kennan, "Foreign Policy and Christian Conscience," *The Atlantic Monthly,* May 1959. Richard B. Gregg, *The Power of Nonviolence.* Nyack, N.Y.: Fellowship Publications, 1959. American Friends Service Committee, *Speak Truth to Power, Quaker Search for an Alternative to Balance.* 1955.
5. George F. Kennan, *loc. cit.,* pp. 44 ff.
6. For a detailed analysis of modern society, cf. my *The Sane Society.* New York: Rinehart and Co., 1955.
7. *SRI Journal,* 1959, vol. 3, p. 140.
8. *Loc. cit.,* p. 52 and p. 65.
9. Peter B. Young, "The Renunciationists," *Airpower,* the Air Force Historical Foundation, vol. VII, no. 1, p. 33.
10. *Ibid.* (My italics; E.F.)
11. Herman Kahn, *Report on a Study of Non-Military Defense.* Rand Corporation, 1958, p. 13.
12. *Ibid.*

The case for
making "just war" possible

BY PAUL RAMSEY

R. PAUL RAMSEY *is Chairman of the Department of Religion at Princeton University. He earned his B.D. and Ph.D. degrees at the Yale University Divinity School and subsequently taught history, social science and philosophy at Millsaps College, social philosophy at Yale, and Christian Ethics at Garrett Theological Seminary, before coming to Princeton in 1944. In 1959-60 he was vice-president of the American Theological Society.*

A teacher and scholar in the field of Christian ethics and social theory, Dr. Ramsey is the author of several volumes and is a frequent contributor of articles to religious and philosophical journals. Among his books are Basic Christian Ethics, War and the Christian Conscience: How Shall Modern War Be Justly Conducted?, *and* Christian Ethics and the Sit-In.

A RECENT editorial in *Worldview*[1] expresses evident dissatisfaction with political "realism" and "prudential" ethics as by no means an adequate contribution of religious ethics to politics in our times. It continues by noting that the nature of modern weapons has given religious pacifists powerful new arguments that have not been adequately answered. It is symptomatic of the ills of religious ethics today, and of political and military doctrine, that the editorial writer gets from the limit he places on "realism" and "prudential" politics to the need for reopening a discussion of pacifism by a quite uncritical rejection of the only genuine alternative there is. He states as a conclusion no one today would think of challenging, that "previous norms for the 'just' war have, for all practical purposes, been rendered obsolete"; and demands that religious leaders find out quickly whether they have anything to say about the destructiveness of modern warfare and not "salve" their "conscience by repeating the ancient rules for a 'just' war—rules which have as much relationship to an all-out modern war as such a war would have to the bow and arrow."[2]

Now obviously, you cannot indict the concept of the just war for drawing up a moral indictment of all-out nuclear warfare as intrinsically immoral; nor should anyone simply dismiss the distinction between the just and the unjust conduct of war because men and nations have the power and are in fact planning to violate this distinction. Too frequently the just war theory is said to be assuredly false or irrelevant or outmoded by people who would not confront the actual policies of their nation with these criteria even if proved true. Translate the traditional terminology distinguishing between just and unjust warfare into contemporary language distinguishing between counter-*forces* and counter-*people* warfare. At once it will be seen that the position that counter-forces warfare alone can be justified for arming the political purposes of a nation may reasonably be proposed as a truth to be acknowledged in military doctrine. It is certainly not irrelevant or anachronistic to say this; and the consciences of men may be not "salved" but awakened if this is said clearly by the moralist and, in collaboration with competent weapons-analysis, concretely *to the point* of the dilemma we confront in modern warfare. The present chapter undertakes an initial step in this direction; first explaining *why,* under the shaping influence of Christian ethics, criteria for just conduct were enunciated by the theory of civilized warfare in the West, and then proceeding to clarify the exact *meaning* of these criteria.

I

It is convenient to begin with a quotation from a Roman Catholic, who is perhaps a "just war" pacifist, concerning "thirteenth century principles . . . as a minimal statement of the Christian ethic," not exhaustive or preclusive of a "higher aim." These principles, writes Robert Hovda "made an exception (that's what it was) to the commandment 'Thou shalt not kill' in the case of a soldier or other military personnel on the opposing (clearly unjust) side in a war. The basis for this exception has been the fact that such a one is cooperating directly in the unjust action of his government and that he is therefore materially if not formally 'guilty.' Generally, moralists extended this exception to include other citizens who were cooperating *directly* in the war effort."[3] However, it is only when the commandment "Thou shalt not kill" is viewed *legalistically,* and only when the actions that are licit or illicit under it are viewed *externally,* that the Christians who formulated the just war theory can be said to have made, in regard to killing another human being, one, single, clearly defined and limited *exception,* and nothing more.

Those persons "formally" directing or participating in the military forces, or "materially" yet closely cooperating in the force that should be repelled and can only be repelled by violent means, these persons are—this theory states—legitimate objects of *direct* violent repression. This conclusion was not only the result of importing into Christian ethics certain conceptions of natural justice from Stoic and other ancient philosophies. Nor did the theory always simply result in a bifurcation of public morality, based on justice, from private morality, based on love—that love which required the early Christians to withdraw altogether from the resistance of evil by political and military means. Instead, intrinsic within the new foundation laid by Christ for the entire conduct of his disciples was the conviction that love and mercy are the fulfilling of the law, of natural justice, and of the meaning expressed in the commandment, "Thou shalt not kill." When in doubt as to the actual action required by this command, one had simply to consult again the requirements of compassion incarnating itself in serving the concrete needs of men. Therefore in the ancient theory of just war, Christian conscience took the form of allowing any killing at all of men for whom Christ died only because military personnel were judged to stand, factually and objectively, at the point where as combatants resistance to them was judged to be necessary in responsibility to many other neighbors. The combatant stood at the point of intersection of many primary claims upon the Christian's life with and for his fellow man.

This still included undiminished fellow humanity with the enemy soldier; yet he was not the only one to take into account. The claims of many others had also to be acknowledged and realistically served in the only way possible. In this world and not some other, faithfulness to all our fellow men, and not only to the enemy, must somehow be enacted. Jesus did not teach that his disciples should lift up the face of another oppressed man to be struck again on the other cheek. Out of neighbor-regarding love for one's fellow men, preferential decision among one's neighbors may and can and should be made. For love's sake (the very principle of the prohibition of killing), and not only for the sake of an abstract justice sovereign over the political realm in separation from the private, Christian thought and action was driven to posit this single "exception" (an exception only when externally viewed): that forces should be repelled and the bearers and close cooperators in military force should be directly repressed, by violent means if necessary, lest many more of God's little ones should be irresponsibly forsaken and lest they suffer more harm than need be. This, then, was not really an "exception," certainly not an arbitrary one; but a determinate expression of justice and mercy. It was an *expression* of the Christian understanding of political responsibility in terms of neighbor-regarding love. It was, and is, a regrettably necessary but still a necessary and morally justifiable expression of our being with and for men, as Christ was *the* man *for* other men. Christian love was the influence that shaped this conclusion. Therefore, the just war theory states not what *may* but what *should* be done. This does not preclude a "higher aim" in personal relations if here one's own goods and life alone are at stake. It does not even preclude higher aims in politics, since as Augustine wrote, "it is a higher glory still to slay war itself with the word than men with the sword, and to procure and maintain peace by peace, not by war." But there can be no higher aim in military affairs, weapons-policy or among the goals of military establishments, except of course the prevention or deterrence of war by means it would be just to fight with.

The criteria by which war was said on occasion to be justifiable in Christian conscience, and military forces or personnel (and close co-operators in mounting the opposing military force) declared to be legitimate objects of direct attack, by the same stroke placed definite limits upon the conduct of war by surrounding *non-combatants* with moral immunity from *direct* attack. Thus, a love-inspired justice going into concrete action fashioned rules for practical conduct—at once justifying war and limiting it. The Christian is commanded to do anything a realistic love commands, and he is prohibited from doing anything for which such love can find no justification. If combatants may and should be resisted directly by violent means to secure a desired and desirable victory, this also requires that non-combatants be never directly assaulted even to that same end. When out of Christian love or from definitions of justice inspired by love it was concluded that the death of an enemy might be directly intended and directly done for the sake of all God's other children within a just or a just endurable political order by which God governs and preserves human life in a fallen world, this also meant that such love could never find sufficient reason for directly intending and directly doing the death of the enemy's children in order to dissuade him from his evil deeds.

Thus, western political thought did not until recently stand clothed only in an "aggressor-defender" concept of warfare, nor did it justify any sort of reply believed to be technically required to stop an aggressor. Warlike action was not justified, until recently, merely by a calculation of the future consequences and choice of the lesser evil in aiming at hypothetical results. Of course, no right action aims at *greater* evil in the results. But this does not mean that every action that prudently aims at good or less evil consequences is therefore right and is to be done. There is also a morality of means, of conduct, or of actions to be put forth. Since at least everyone seeks peace and desires justice, the *ends* for which wars may legitimately be fought are not nearly so im-

portant in the theory of the just war as is the moral and political
wisdom contained in its reflection upon the *conduct* or means of
warfare. Unless there is a morality applicable to instruments of war
and intrinsically limiting its conduct, then we must simply admit that
war has no limits—since these can hardly be derived from "peace" as
the "final cause" of just wars. Since it was for the sake of the innocent
and helpless ones that the Christian first thought himself obliged to
make war against an enemy whose objective deeds were judged to be
evil and in need of restraint by any feasible means, how could he ever
conclude from this that it was permitted him to destroy some "innocents" for the sake of other "innocents" closer to him in natural or
social affinity? Thus was twin-born the justification of war and its
limitation by the moral immunity of non-combatants (and the immunity of *remote* material cooperators in the force which should and
had to be repelled).

This states *why* the theory of justifiable warfare was developed in
the Christian West.* Whether this theory has any longer any bearing
upon the conduct of nations is, however, a question that cannot be
answered without first gaining a more complete and accurate understanding of the meaning of the norms expressed in terms of the
ancient theory. Nothing can be more irresponsible, and less condu-
cive to disciplined reflection in an area today sorely in need of being
subjected to rational control, than to dismiss the just war theory on a

---

* Here one must simply voice sharp disagreement with Hans J. Morgenthau
("The Demands of Prudence," *Worldview,* vol. 3, no. 6, June, 1960, pp. 6-7). It is
not the case that "the natural aspirations proper to the political sphere—and there
is no difference in kind between domestic and international politics—contravene
by definition the demands of the Christian ethics," or that "it is *a priori* impossible for political man to be at the same time a good politician—complying with
the rules of political conduct—and to be a good Christian—complying with the
demands of Christian ethics." The just war theory bridged the "unbridgeable
gulf" Morgenthau thinks he sees. Its genesis shows that, as Christian ethics goes
into actual practice, it fashions and shapes itself into principles for the direction
of concrete action. Of course, no proposal for the *direction* or guidance of action
can be a simple factual summary of the context in which that action is to be put
forth. Only for the most abstract versions of natural law, however, is it true to
say: "The gap between the rational postulates of natural law and the contingencies of the concrete situation within which man must act and judge is just as
wide as the gulf which separates the demands of Christian ethics from the rules
of political action. In truth, . . . both gaps are identical." If that is the meaning

mistaken understanding of it—as often happens today, from different points of view, by political realists and by resurgent pacifism. To come to terms with these terms will be our next undertaking.

II

In order to comprehend the meaning of "non-combatancy," it is necessary to understand a number of primary notions or distinctions fundamental in the traditional moral rules for the just conduct of war. The following may be cited as most important: (1) The distinction between "formal" and only "material," and between "close" and "remote," cooperation in the force that should be repelled. (2) The distinction between the "guilty" who are legitimate targets of violent repression and the "innocent" who are not. These are very misleading terms, since their meaning is exhaustively stated under the first contrast, and is reducible to degrees of actual participation in hostile force. (3) The distinction between "direct" and "indirect" attack. It was never supposed that non-combatants were morally immune from indirect injury or death on however colossal a scale, if there is proportionate grave reason for doing this. This has sometimes been expressed by saying that death to the innocent may be "permitted" to result "accidentally" from an act of war primarily directed against military forces. But if the word "accident" is used, it is in a philosophical or technical sense, and not with its usual meaning. For the "permitted" killing of non-combatants does not just happen to take place. It is foreknown, and foreknown to result as a necessary effect of the same action that causes the death of political leaders or military personnel who are its legitimate targets. This brings us to (4) the analysis of acts

---

of the natural law, then it must be insisted that the theory of just conduct in war had nothing to do with it, but arose rather from a concretely oriented Christian love in-principling itself in responsible ways to serve actual man within the fabric of political life and institutions. Not without further examination should we agree with Morgenthau that, in the political sphere, man "is precluded from acting morally" and "the best he can do is to minimize the intrinsic immorality of the political act" (by choosing "the lesser evil"), or that "the best man is capable of is to be guided by the vision of a life lived in compliance with the Christian code and to narrow the gap between his conduct and that code." All this presupposes an asserted gap—between Christian ethics and politics, or between natural law and political decision—which the criteria of just action in war asserts it has at least partly bridged—not leaving the entire leap to techof war as (like many other human actions) having double or multiple effects, and to the so-called "rule of double effect." The latter requires that a distinction be made between (a) killing that is directly intended (in the subjective order) and directly done (in the objective, physical order) and (b) killing that is only permitted even if it is *indirectly* done (i.e. also *caused*) by the same action that causes the death of men who are its primary targets. Acts of war which directly intend and directly effect the death of non-combatants are to be classed morally with murder, and are never excusable. If the excuse is that victory requires this, then we would be saying that the end justifies an intrinsically wrong means or that men may be murdered in order to do good. A desired and desirable victory may, however, justify conduct in warfare that causes the death, and is foreknown to cause the death, of non-combatants *indirectly*. This would *not* be directly to do evil that good may come of it. There is a significant moral difference between the destruction in obliteration warfare which is deliberately wanton and murderous, and the destruction and death that is among the tragic consequences of counter-*forces* warfare. This distinction is not determined by the amount of the devastation or the number of deaths, but by the direction of the action itself, i.e. by what is deliberately intended and directly done. This permits there to be foreseeable evil consequences acceptable among the multiple effects of military action.

Whether these latter effects are acceptable, or not, must be assessed by prudential reason balancing good and evil, or lesser evil, consequences. But first one should be able to discriminate between acts of murder and acts of war. Indiscriminate bombing or counter-people warfare stands indicted as intrinsically wrong. In this sense, multi-megaton weapons are "morally unshootable." To use them would be

---

nical reason or to that prudence to which Morgenthau appeals. Finally, it should be pointed out that Morgenthau's view that the gap can be cut down, not by any shaping of principles of political conduct, but only by the strategy of choosing the lesser evil, under the "vision" of a life lived otherwise, places him in the position of not being able even to understand correctly John Courtney Murray's remark that nuclear weapons are "from the moral point of view . . . unshootable." That, he says, is "because of the consequences of shooting them." This chapter will demonstrate that this is only the *last* reason (while a sufficient one) for calling multi-megaton weapons morally unshootable.

the direct murder of the innocent as a means of victory. This, however, does not condemn every enlargement of legitimate military targets in the course of weapons-development, much less the *unavoidable* enlargement of the indirect effects of counter-forces warfare. Multi-megaton weapons may also be "unshootable" in this second sense: because we are, in the last place, forced to conclude that there can be no greater evil than the *consequences* of using them. Therefore, after having permitted and prohibited actions by an analysis of the intrinsic nature of each, it has yet to be determined whether military action lawful in itself should actually be done. This requires (5) a prudential estimate of the consequences to see whether there is in the good effect sufficiently grave reason for also indirectly producing the evil effect. Thus, the traditional morality of war locates in the last place a calculus of probability and a morality of the ends in view. In the end, proper place should be given to sitting down to count the costs of a proposed action. While an effect cannot justify any means, one effect can justify another effect because of the greater good or "lesser evil" in one than in the other.

In recent years, bellicists and pacifists have united to declare that every act of war as such is intrinsically immoral. These alike declare the just war theory no longer applicable—bellicists, to the end of engaging in war without moral limitations; pacifists, to withdraw from it altogether; and many so-called Christian realists, with moderation placed only upon the political objectives for which, they say, wars should ever be fought (and *through* the ends, upon the means). In order for either of these parties to make a beginning toward reaching one of these conclusions, it is first of all necessary for them to misunderstand the criteria for the conduct of war and the rules of civilized warfare. Terms are used imprecisely in order to discredit the quite precise notions of the moral doctrine of war that has prevailed in western history. Therefore, the concept of "noncombatancy" has not been proved wrong by sound moral or political or military analysis. It has been rejected before having been understood. Thus, the traditional analysis of the morality of war has been thoughtlessly rejected, and the necessary totality of modern war largely conceded.

How can the "facts" of warfare between modern industrial and metropolitan societies prove that there are now no non-combatants when this conclusion depends in every respect upon whether we have in our heads such notions as the moral significance of the degrees of proximity or remoteness of cooperation in unjust aggression, and the distinction between direct and indirect killing? Too often in Protestant and in secular writings on the subject of morality and war it is also erroneously supposed that *direct* killing is the only kind of killing sought to be justified; and so it has come to be an unquestioned maxim that, for war to be justly conducted, non-combatants have to be clearly and in detail distinguishable from combatants. Moreover, we would have to be sure not only *who* these people are but also that *where* they live is not within or near any legitimate target area, and that none will be slain or injured as an unavoidable indirect consequence of direct military action. As a result of faulty analysis of the morality of war, if today the moral immunity of non-combatants from direct attack is not simply ignorantly ridiculed, the nullity of it is assumed as a premise rather than as a conclusion to be reached by disciplined moral reflection. On this understanding of the matter, any act of war is either an immorality to be done out of military necessity or an immorality never to be done out of Christian love; and there are no significant moral distinctions to be made among warring actions except between those that succeed and those that do not succeed in obtaining victory, or between means that are proportionate and those disproportionate to the end of victory.

Plainly, it is necessary for most people to come to terms again with the terms of the ancient limits of civilized warfare. It is the *concept* of non-combatancy that has first been jettisoned from our minds; and this has happened because the *concept* of degrees of cooperation, the *concept* justifying the repulsion of objectively "guilty" forces as well as those "formally" or personally responsible for their direction, the *concept* of an indirect yet unavoidable and foreknown effect alongside the legitimately intended effects of military action, or the *concept* of double effects flowing from the same neutral or good action as cause, bringing along with the good result also a tragically necessary evil consequence in the limited, not directly intended, yet foreseen destruction of civilian life (still not the same as wholesale murder)— all these notions have eroded from the minds of men. *This,* then, is the reason we are prey to the illusion that modern industrial society has completely changed the nature of warfare, and that not simply mass defection from sound moral reasoning has rendered wholly inapplicable or indeed senseless any attempt to conduct war in accordance with the carefully constructed concepts of traditional Christian morality. Of course, non-combatants are not in modern society roped off like spectators at a medieval tournament. In the theory of just war they never had to be. We only have to know *that* there are babies among the civilian population of any enemy nation, we do not even have to know that there are any grown men and women deserving to be classed as non-combatants in order to know *with certainty* that warfare should be force-counter-forces warfare, and calculated attack be limited to legitimate military targets. There are many people, other than infants, going about their little human affairs whom a loving justice should surround with immunity limiting violence; and to know this we do not need to know *who* or *where* they are. This moral limit still holds, even if it had to be admitted that responsible political and military action must now place civilians with their moral immunity from direct attack in far greater danger even in a justly conducted war than ever before in human history, because (it might be asserted) there are many more legitimate targets than ever before and because the firepower of even a just war and the indirect effects of even its right conduct have enormously increased.

The difference between justifiable and wholly unjustifiable warfare can perhaps be better grasped from an examination of some current mistakes. In modern warfare, it is said, "all human and material resources are mobilized," and only "small children and the helpless sick and the aged stand outside the war effort . . . Total war, in this sense of the involvement of the whole nation in it, cannot be avoided if we have a major war at all."[4] Now, who ever defined a "non-combatant" in such a fashion, as one who "stands outside" of any relation to his nation's action? Who ever meant by a non-combatant a person who, to be one, would have to be utterly helpless, and incapable of any activity at all with important results for the common weal? Evident in such an undiscriminating definition of the "involvement" of a whole nation in war is no conception of the significance of degrees of remoteness or closeness of cooperation in a nation's war effort such as was essential in any definition of the moral immunity of non-combatants in the past. The foregoing statement, therefore, constitutes no objection at all to the application of the moral rules of warfare even in the case of two modern industrial societies locked in a war of attrition. Even more can it be said to have no force at all to nullify the distinction between counter-forces and counter-people warfare with present and future weapons which insure that wars will be fought quickly and not out of inventories. That brief period of western history when counter-*factory* warfare was supposed to justify counter-*people* warfare has now come to an abrupt end.

The traditional distinction between combatant and non-combatant, it is asserted, today is "far less clear" than in the past. Evident here is no conception of the fact that, in the moral choice between direct and indirect killing of civilians, or between counter-forces and indiscriminate counter-retaliatory warfare, this distinction *does not need to be clear*. We do not need to know *who* or *where* the non-combatants are in order to know that indiscriminate bombing exceeds the moral limits of warfare that can ever barely be justified. We have only to know *that* there are non-combatants—even "only small children and the helpless sick and the aged"—in order to know the basic moral difference between limited and total war.

This same mistake, in my opinion, was made by Professor John Bennett, who ordinarily writes with discernment upon this subject. "It has become increasingly difficult," he writes, "to distinguish in detail between combatants and non-combatants and sometimes the teaching about the just war has been legalistic at this point, if we grant that the use of military force is ever justified at all."[5] That unexamined statement is not worth having; and upon examining it two remarks should be made: (a) *Careful* statements as to the just conduct of war ought not to be dismissed out of hand as "legalistic." (b) To prohibit the *direct* killing (while allowing the *indirect* killing) of non-combatants, it is not at all necessary to distinguish them "in detail." We have only to know that anyone is there—children, the aged, the sick, barbers, cobblers, and Latin school teachers among the people we intend to obliterate by "enlarging the target." We only have to know that there are any civilians, whose lives are made the *intended, direct* object of violence, who are not now closely supporting the military force it would be just and necessary to resist by force limited to this.

We are told that it is now "practically impossible to distinguish between guilty and innocent. Certainly men who are drafted into uniform may be among the least guilty."[6] Who ever clothed non-combatants with moral immunity from direct attack by first investigating their innocence in the highest subjective and personal sense? Who ever declared combatants (or the "guilty") to be legitimate objects of direct attack or counter-attack simply because, unlike mercenaries in the past or men drafted today into "democratic" armies, they are more personally guilty than the rest of their countrymen? The statement that conscript armies, made up of men who may not wish to kill, are *therefore* made up of men who are not *unjust* aggressors and give no one the right to kill them, assumes that the point was to prove the guilt of combatants in a fully personal sense. Against this stands the notion of objective or functional guilt because of status in the forces that should be repelled. Against this stands also the fact that for many centuries after participation in war was said to be justified for Christian conscience, it still was never allowed that, when one's own life or goods alone were at stake, the evil intention of a clearly guilty assailant gave the Christian any right to resist or wound or kill him whom by his wounds and death Christ came to save. No amount or kind of guilt in the fully personal sense as such gave any man the intrinsic right to kill another. Instead, the permission and the duty to do this arose because of the place where the bearer of hostile force stood in relation to God's other children, and to their need to be served by Christians, if at all, in the existing order of the common life by the maintenance of a tolerable justice for them.

This demonstrates, it seems to me, that in rejecting as invalid the quite discriminating concepts of the just war theory, all too many people have first employed insufficiently articulated terms, or blockbuster concepts, all to the end of obliterating the moral wisdom deposited in the traditional view of the morality of war. No wonder, then, that we were morally ready to use blockbusters, and now metropolisbusters, in actual fact! War first became total in the minds of men. Why this happened among religious people, who should have remembered their traditions and who should cultivate conceptual clarity in moral analysis, can perhaps be partly explained by the effort to persuade the pacifists, as World War II approached, that in no way could they avoid "contributing to the war effort." Pacifist Christians may have been wrong in the religious and political judgments they made in refusing direct participation in war; but they were certainly not wrong in discerning a significant distinction between civilian and combatant status. (Pacifists make this distinction *for themselves* and *their own* society, while refusing to make the same necessary distinction between the people and forces of the enemy, which entails acceptance of positive responsibility to resist the latter by military means.) On this distinction hangs the discrimination between war and murder, between limited and unlimited war, between barely civilized and wholly uncivilized, even if technically efficient, military action.

At stake also in this discrimination is not only the defense of civilization against total war, but against totalitarianism as well. In stating so blandly that practically no one "stands outside" the war effort and no one is "innocent" and there is no one who may not be directly killed for some good cause, have we not in principle included practically everyone, to the whole extent of his being, within the direction of the common life toward political goals? When men wage wars if they must and do not maintain a relation *of non-relation,* or remote relation, between the civilian life of a nation and its fighters, they have already in principle totally politicized human life. So much is at stake in restoring the laws of civilized warfare, of fighting, if we must, in a just manner for the preservation of just orders of life. Anything else is technically efficient barbarism, no matter what "values" may be our objectives or the names we use, like fig leaves, to cover our unseemly acts.

The Dun Report which we have been following, rejects, of course, "war in which all moral restraints are thrown aside and all the purposes of the community are fully controlled by sheer military expedience." The question is whether the "moral restraints" not to be thrown aside have sufficient substance and careful enough articulation to provide any guidance for the military conduct of nations. A consequentialist ethics limits means only by subordinating them to limited and just ends. "Moral restraints" are placed mainly upon wanton killing or a savagery that kills without reckoning. Thus, it is pointed out that some methods of fighting "cause more pain and maiming without commensurate military decisiveness. Some are more indiscriminate ... We cannot, therefore, be released from the responsibility for doing no more hurt than must be." Now, we have seen that the church's teaching about morality and warfare calls—in the last place—for a prudential calculation of consequences that may be expected to follow from inherently lawful, right or indifferent action. The proportionately greater good or lesser evil in one effect of such action must justify producing a lesser evil effect, or else the action, in itself licit, ought never to be done. But in the above statement this principle of proportionality, or the prudential balancing of effects, stands almost entirely alone in determining the meaning of "indiscriminate" or wanton action.[7]* One should not kill without "reckoning"; and in the main he reckons only the consequences.

Robert L. Calhoun's objection to this was to the point: "The norm of practically effective inhibition turns out to be, after all, military decisiveness; and beyond ruling out wanton destructiveness, Christian conscience in wartime seems to have chiefly the effect (certainly important but scarcely decisive) of making Christians do reluctantly what military necessity requires."[8] After all, manuals enunciating standards for the Housing, Care and Surgical Handling of Laboratory Animals rule out of bounds the use of methods that cause laboratory rats more pain and maiming without commensurate medical or scientific decisiveness; and they are quite prepared to lay down the moral law that no one engaged in medical research can "be released from the responsibility for doing no more hurt than must be." Clearly, a political morality that focuses on motives or ends only, and gives over entirely to prudence and judgments of utility the determination of the way and means to these goals, has already reduced human beings to the level of creatures to be managed and controlled in any way that may be believed to be commensurate with the attainment of political and military goals. While one should not do people more damage than need be, and with proper motives and objectives, still on such a view they are already merely and wholly *means*.

A different estimate of the Dun Report as a whole might be reached if the principle of proportionality were not so central in determining the "sense" in which it says Christians have to reject total war—if, in

---

* Cf. pp. 13 and 14 of Dun Report, *op. cit.*: "The real moral line between what may be done and what may not be done by the Christian lies not in the realm of the distinction between weapons but in the realm of the *motives* for using and the *consequences* of using all kinds of weapons . . . We have found no moral distinction between these instruments of warfare, apart from the *ends* they serve and the *consequences* of their use" (italics added). But between motives, on the one hand, and ends and consequences, on the other, stands the nature of the *act* itself, which may be moral or immoral; and this too is not *primarily* a discrimination among weapons as such.

other words, another clear statement in this Report could be regarded as still more fundamental in the logic of its moral argument. For there are said to be "real distinctions . . . to illumine and help conscience in its trouble"; "the destruction of life clearly incidental to the destruction of decisive military objectives, for example, is radically different from mass destruction which is aimed primarily at the lives of civilians, their morale, or the sources of their livelihood." If this judment had been placed first, and fundamental to all other considerations, a different evaluation of this Report would be required. This would be to say that we may be decisively prohibited from calculating the military decisiveness of *some* proposed acts of war in an attempt to justify them from their supposed results. Instead, the judgment just cited is given as an "example"; and it is immediately followed by the conclusion that "in the event of war, Christian conscience guides us to restraint from destruction *not essential to our total objectives.*"[9] That obviates entirely the distinction between counter-forces and counter-people warfare; and it provides little "guidance" toward the limitation or alteration of the shape warfare has assumed in the present day.

Professor John Bennett, to whom critical reference has already been made, gave clear utterance to the criteria for the just conduct of war when he wrote that "the use of weapons to slaughter civilian populations, recklessness in regard to future generations, and the destruction of the fabric of national community and of civilized life are opposed to all that the churches have taught in the past." Concerning massive deterrence, he asks: "Should deterrent power be thought of as directed against the opponent's power to strike or against the whole population in the hope of deterring the will to strike? If the latter is the objective, we are again in the realm of unlimited terror and unlimited striking power and an unlimited arms race. If the former is the objective there may be a better chance to avoid the errors that result from panic. Also the former objective raises a less acute moral conflict than the latter. Do we know what the present presuppositions of the U.S. government are on this matter?"[10]

Perhaps the following comment should be made concerning Bennett's summary of the moral limits upon warfare in terms of prohibiting "the destruction of the fabric of national community and of civilized life" in the enemy nation; and upon his judgment that warring action is "intrinsically evil" when it "takes as its target of attack, whether intentionally or not, the recuperative powers of the enemy" or the "fabric of national community" in a nation at war.[11]* Such formulations of the criteria for the just conduct of war are of considerable worth. Certainly Christians and just men should have regard for the uniqueness of the various peoples of the world in their traditions, ways of life and distinct contributions to the enrichment of mankind. The nations also are creations of God; and the world would be poorer without any one of these creatures of His.

Yet, it seems clear that such statements of the principles that should limit warfare are *reducible* to the more fundamental principles surrounding civilian life with moral immunity from direct repression. It is to be feared that, unless this reduction is carried out with conceptual clarity in the analysis of morality and warfare, we have not yet elaborated the firmest possible moral guard against total war. Moreover, it seems to me that Christian love, expressed in principles of justice that suit it, does not first of all fashion itself in terms of regard for the fabric of community life, nor does Christian faith, going into political action, take effect primarily in fidelity to the recuperative powers of an enemy nation. Not nations but first persons are elevated to citizenship in another City and to a destiny kept between themselves and God which prohibits any man from reducing them wholly to the status of means useful in attaining some historical goal in the life of the kingdoms of this world. The neighbors and companions God has given us are primarily persons, within the separate national traditions He has provided for them and for us. Bennett's way of articulating the point at which the conduct of war becomes intrinsically unjust seems clearly derivative. Logically and Christianly, it is predicated upon the claims and obligations pointed out in the traditional doctrine. At most, it is an articulation that helpfully supplements the ancient formulas.

The just war theory cannot be repealed; it can only be violated. It states the limit beyond which war as such becomes in itself a wholly non-human and non-political activity, and the point beyond which military force becomes senseless violence, and our weapons no longer weapons of *war*. This is not because war has an "essence" or "nature" but because man has; and because political society has a nature to which military means must be kept subordinate. The distinction be-

* Strike "whether intentionally or not," since an intrinsic *moral* evil cannot be without intention.

tween "combatants" and "non-combatants" asserts that there is both some relation between a civil society and its fighters and yet non-relation or remote relation between them. The maintenance of this distinction, or of this distance and subordination in the relation of combatants to the society they defend, is of the very essence of war that may under any circumstances be chosen by men who have not wholly lost all political morality and their political reasons. Push-buttons may be able to launch retaliatory and counter-retaliatory warfare, but political man with all his faculties in exercise cannot do any such purposeless deed.

The problem today is "just war," limited war. This is not a discription of the facts, opposed to other descriptions. It is rather an imperative statement, a political imperative which points the way in which alone, through intelligent moral action in direction of national policy, warfare can be enclosed again within the political purposes of nations from which it has escaped. This is the case for making just war possible. There is more to be gained from a concerted effort to make just war possible than from attempting to "prevent" war without first (or also) altering the shape it now has in reality and, first of all, in the minds of men.

III

Exactly how counter-forces warfare can again be made possible cannot be fully explained here. In fact, no moralist alone should undertake to do this, since that is primarily the task of the weapons-analyst and the statesman in shaping policy under the guidance and in the context of the regulative criteria for the purposive conduct of war. Nevertheless some concluding remarks[12] may be addressed to the astonishing fact that the just war theory still appears outmoded and irrelevant to an age that gives the name of "realism" to proposals that are more "out of *this* world" than the reflections of any medieval theologian upon the morality of war.

Some say: hard verification standards must be included in any arms control or other agreement, until an open society is here.* Others say:

* Thus Edward Teller opposes the suspension of nuclear tests without the most stringent enforcement of the agreement by inspection. At the same time he writes that "the idea of massive retaliation is impractical and immoral," that responding to evil with much greater evil is "contrary to our sense of justice"; and he calls for *limited* nuclear war to be designed, the limit on size and targets to be deter-

soft verification because an open world of peace loving peoples is already immanent.* These opposites meet in their common expectation that force can be banished from human history. No wonder the more realistic just war theory is overlooked!

Less obviously is this still the assumption behind current policies for the deterrence of war by means of apparently hardheaded schemes for stabilizing (while maintaining) counter-people deterrence. We need to look briefly at proposals that would make weapons of reprisal "invulnerable" by submarine and other means of mobility, and then base arms control and the prevention of war (i.e. the *unjust* war built into such weapons-plans) upon the "stabilization" of this system. Such will undoubtedly be the military posture of the United States in the '60's; and some of the best intelligences in this country have devoted themselves to the solution of the problem of how current technological developments in the weapons field can simply be moulded into invulnerable, stable systems. A statesman today needs to ponder long upon the essentials of any such proposal, and meditate upon it, perhaps as if in a reverie.

If President Kennedy sits down with the recent Arms Control issue of *Daedalus*, before he can say "Second Inaugural" he might with a little imagination tell himself the following tale as a symbol for the present world situation with which statesmanship must deal. Down in

---

mined, apparently, only by what "best serves the military purpose of that conflict." This affords no *decisive* limit upon ever increasing firepower directed against populations. How, may we ask, can a man alive today endure this prospect? The answer is: Teller's faith is built on nothing less than a quite utopian hope, namely, that a world of "open" societies can be achieved in time, "freedom to exchange information" be "guaranteed by enforceable international law," secretiveness become reprehensible, and "a strong and widespread condemnation of all practices of secrecy may in the long run have a strong effect even on those countries which value this form of security most." Can any proposal be more apolitical in today's world? If "a gradual and well-planned abandonment" of secrecy can claim to be a realistic and relevant proposal, even more can be claimed for a plan of graduated, unilateral steps to make counter-forces warfare possible (Edward Teller, "The Feasibility of Arms Control and the Principle of Openness," *Daedalus* [later published in book form by George Braziller, Inc.], Fall, 1960, pp. 792, 794, 795, 797. Cf.: ". . . For arms control to succeed, secrecy among nations must become disreputable" [Ithiel de Sola Pool, "Public Opinion and the Control of Armaments," *Daedalus,* Fall, 1960, p. 995]).

* In contrast to Teller, those who believe that an agreement to cease testing should be negotiated with less rigorous verification, and who rely on this as a step toward

the mountains of Tennessee where for decades there has been fun and feuding, the Hatfields and the McCoys suddenly one day found themselves in a most extraordinary posture toward one another. High up on one ridge, the eldest Hatfield discovered in the sights of his rifle the youngest McCoy gurgling in a cradle, while at the very same moment the eldest McCoy on the opposite ridge draws deadly aim at the youngest Hatfield lying on a quilt on the porch. Each knows, and knows that the other knows, that this is the case. For some weeks that seem a very long time indeed, each tries to improve his situation by calling on all the other Hatfields and McCoys to come and station themselves at various places in the hills, each aiming at the last human life on the other side. The deterrence is truly "massive"; and if this system is ever used it will have failed completely. It looks as if effective feuding has been abolished. Such has long been the desire of the few sentimental ones born from time to time in both families; and now technology has achieved what religion never could. While the lion and the lamb have not exactly lain down together, the Hatfields and the McCoys seem capable of forever standing there together, since each sustains the other and prevents his firing. This is in effect a condition, it is supposed, equivalent to mutual total disarmament. Since neither could fight if he wanted to he cannot want to. This seems so clear that strategists on both sides have declared that not so

---

further agreements that may control war and armaments without changing their present shape, often provide themselves with other exits into another world than this. This may be the world rule of law, world government, a world without war, a world in which nations can't fight if they want to and can't want to; or, short of these achievements, "people" inspection. The latter means that it is thought that the West should accept fewer inspection stations and fewer veto-free on-the-spot inspections because, in negotiating such an agreement, it may be possible for every nation to become "entrapped" in its own propaganda, leading to an "increase in the probability that some individual or individuals will identify with the inspectors instead of with their government and will expose illicit activity." Ideally, we know the kind of propaganda which will make a government most completely a prisoner of its own moral leadership in the cause of international peace through arms control or general disarmament; and which tends to perfect the system of "people" detection: "The propaganda which will make cheating hardest is propaganda in which a nation's top officials repeatedly tell their people that it is their duty to cooperate with an arms control and inspection system." (Ithiel de Sola Pool, "Public Opinion and the Control of Armaments," *Daedalus,* Fall, 1960, pp. 989-990.) The world in which we live, however, is one in which the Russian negotiator, upon the resumption of the test negotiations in March, 1961, renounced

many guns are needed; that one has only to be able to deliver unacceptable damage; that "over-kill" is not needed; and that a finite amount of deterrence is enough, while the rest of society can devote itself to chewing sugar cane and making moonshine whiskey (the obvious ends of policy: consumer goods).

Nevertheless the gunners on both sides begin to quake with fear because they realize this system of deterrence is quite unstable. Apart from the danger of an accidental outbreak of hostilities, each side begins to suspect that the other may launch a surprise attack or pre-empt against the launching of his own surprise attack, which pre-emption in turn would have to be pre-empted, etc. Mutual "anticipatory retaliation" is always about to take over control of the system which was supposed to unarm both sides. This is not because both sides are in danger of miscalculating but in danger of calculating *correctly*. Meantime it has become apparent that ordinary feuding has not been deterred. Under the umbrella of deterrence, the grown Hatfield and McCoy boys continue fighting whenever there seems an opportunity to increase their power-control of the valley in face of any weakness in conventional forces. Each time this occurs, Hatfield says firmly, "No one should doubt our resolution"; and McCoy exclaims, "We will bury you." The side wins which acts as if it is the more capable of wholly irrational action, since each knows that the system exceeds any of the reasonable purposes feuding ever had. War has actually not been abolished; we have only attempted to exceed it. And the side most bemused by this possibility loses in every encounter of real power.

---

his country's former agreement that an inspection system be under a single director and proposed instead a three-man inspectorate composed of Communist, Western and Neutralist representatives in which Russia would have a veto; and this is a world in which what the Russians call "control without disarmament" already seems to them to be barely disguised espionage (cf. Wm. R. Frye, "Characteristics of Recent Arms Control Proposals and Agreements," *Daedalus,* Fall, 1960, p. 741; and Jerome B. Wiesner, "Comprehensive Arms-Limitation Systems," *Daedalus,* Fall, 1960, pp. 920-921). Moreover, "the Soviets undoubtedly look on their secrecy as a military asset. In allowing it to be pierced by inspection, they consider they are making a separate, or additional, sacrifice of their military potential" (Robert R. Bowie, "Basic Requirements of Arms Control," *Daedalus,* Fall, 1960, p. 714).

In the midst of the threat that weapons will be mobilized into use (out of mutual fear of surprise attack), technological changes take place which seem capable of abolishing surprise attack itself—without, however, removing the immobilization of politics and the confusion and partial immobilization of ordinary feuding and fighting as an extension of purposive policy, especially among the peace-loving Hatfields. A way is found to harden and protect the guns. The gunners begin to move around, so that you don't know where they are. The bases are placed on mobile railroad cars, planes, barges, and submarines (Polaris). The retaliatory forces are made *invulnerable* to surprise attack. While still aimed at baby Hatfield and baby McCoy,* counter-*people* warfare seems miraculously to have been transformed into counter-*forces* warfare. Only counter-*forces* war seems now to be possible since it would be necessary for either side first to find a way of getting at the other side's guns before using his own in the way originally intended (or in the way it was originally intended that by them the other side would be deterred from using his in the way *he* originally intended). Plans for "cooperating with the enemy" in tacit agreements to maintain the mutual "invulnerability" of deterrence, and arms control schemes to "stabilize" the deterrent gain wide currency, especially among the Hatfields.

After this flight of fancy, our statesman may have some sober thoughts that will cut athwart basing national policy on any such expectation. While still daydreaming and before altogether returning to the real world, he might even reflect for one moment as a moralist. If so, he will conclude that it would be totally immoral to "stabilize" the deterrent and "prevent" war by such means without fundamentally altering its present shape *even if this succeeded*. Still somewhat in the mood for myth-making, he might suppose that one Labor Day weekend no one was killed or maimed on the highways; and that the reason for the remarkable restraint placed on the reck-

---

* In fact the danger they are in has been *increased:* The oceanic system is an "improvement" over land-based missiles not only because invulnerable to surprise attack and not only because it can make for a measured response; but also because the smaller warhead on submarine-based missiles, "with possibly a lesser degree of accuracy as compared with ground-based missiles, makes them *less of a threat to the enemy's retaliatory forces and more of a genuine deterrent*" (i.e. more useful only in reprisals against populations. T. C. Schelling, "Reciprocal Measures for Arms Stabilization," *Daedalus*, Fall, 1960, p. 905).

lessness of automobile drivers was that suddenly every one of them discovered he was driving with a baby tied to his front bumper! That would be no way to regulate traffic *even if it succeeds* in regulating it perfectly, since such a system makes innocent human lives the *direct object* of attack and uses them as a mere *means* for restraining the drivers of automobiles. It would even have to be assumed that the drivers will tacitly agree never to remove the baby from the bumper, since that would destabilize the entire system of controls! Against such a proposal it obviously should be said that restraints and penalties ought to be objectively brought to bear only upon *the drivers* of automobiles, even if this means the abandonment of the hope of saving the lives of every human being (guilty and innocent alike) who venture upon the highways on any holiday weekend. The rational and only just thing to do, if we wish no longer to accept the necessity of the number of deaths that repeatedly take place in the face of vain moral injunctions to drive carefully, would be to introduce basic changes into the machines that are driven, by compulsory safety devices and built-in maximum speeds of forty miles an hour, and enforce with heavier penalties the laws defining the proper conduct of drivers.

But in the real world of political and military encounters, the question is: *can* any scheme hope to succeed which accepts retaliatory strategies directed against populations, and only tries to stabilize these deterrent forces and perfect the mutual invulnerability of counter-people weapons? It would have to be tacitly agreed that baby Hatfield and baby McCoy will not be protected directly, and a piece of sheet-metal never be placed between them and the bullets. A successful civil defense program on either side of the valley would not be impossible so much as it would be undesirable, for to succeed in protecting the last possible survivors of such defense plans if they are ever used would be destabilizing to the very system calculated to prevent its having to be used (always without any basic alteration in the design itself of war and defense). Here, the morality of the matter insists on obtruding, for this defines what is politically wrong in all such products of man's artistic, technical reason in designing weapons, arms control and deterrence systems. No government can *effectively communicate* to its people the fact that it is accepting the complete reversal of a proper relation between a nation and its armament. It cannot tell them, so that they feel it along their pulses, that old ladies and children are now the "fighters" to be maneuvered into position in the struggle for national advantage;* that civil defense is a weapon that perhaps should not be used; that a "race" in shelter programs might be exceedingly dangerous and the Russians may even now be mounting this in a clandestine manner;** that it is *the arms* alone that can be and are now sought to be protected, and not the nation; and that it is essential to this that precisely the people generally be left with no protection.

Moreover, task forces of Hatfields and McCoys are already at work out in the woodshed developing anti-gunnery gunnery (anti-submarine warfare† and anti-missile missiles††). Their barns are said to contain stores of bacteriological, chemical and radiological weapons. These capabilities for total war cannot of themselves be miraculously transformed into counter-forces weapons. Nothing will automatically insure that germs will have first to be let loose on the forces of an enemy bearing these same weapons before one would dare use them in civilian reprisal. Not only in active defense but in offensive plans as well may there be an upsetting scientific breakthrough that will make vulnerable every supposed invulnerable system of deterrence and destabilize any system of supposedly stable arms control erected upon the preservation and use of counter-*people* warfare (or its use for deterrence). ". . . We are having a complete technological revolution

* ". . . In the kilomegaton age evacuation of cities may have replaced general mobilization as the most provocative step short of war that a nation can take." (Arthur T. Hadley, *The Nation's Safety and Arms Control.* New York: The Viking Press, 1961, p. 29.)
** ". . . The Russians must be watched closely. For should the Soviets start a massive shelter program, America must immediately respond." (Arthur T. Hadley, *The Nation's Safety and Arms Control.* New York: The Viking Press, 1961, p. 102.) To build shelters would give little protection, but it would "permit a surprise attacker to remove his hostages" (*ibid.,* p. 101).
† President Kennedy, in his first military budget message, did *not* omit anti-submarine warfare from his expanded emphasis on non-nuclear weapons, while at the same time counting heavily on the supposed invulnerability of our own Polaris submarines from Soviet attack (*The New York Times,* March 29, 1961).
†† "It is important to note that a missile deterrent system would be unbalanced by the development of a highly effective anti-missile defense system and *if it appears possible to develop one, the agreement should explicitly prohibit the development and deployment of such systems*" (Jerome B. Wiesner, "Comprehensive Arms-Limitation Systems," *Daedalus,* Fall, 1960, p. 935; italics added).

in the art of war approximately every five years. . . . Technological progress is so rapid that there are almost bound to be doctrinal lags,"[13] in any of the proposed schemes for subduing our galloping war-technology *only by means of that technology itself* without any decision to alter the weapons themselves. Exposed to view is the fact that the Hatfields and the McCoys cannot make war or *make defense* in any such fashion that accepts as its premise a fundamental reversal of the subordinate relation of arms to the fabric of a nation's life and its purposive policies. Faced with such manifold difficulties, it would seem that the eldest Hatfield (if he is a realist) would rather make some gesture in the direction of indicating to McCoy that he is willing to lower his rifle and direct his aim upon the *forces* opposing him and not upon the babies. Graduated steps to make just war possible would seem to contain as much or more promise than delicate schemes for attempting to stabilize the altogether extraordinary and fluid situation in which one now finds himself as head of a powerful feuding family.

Moreover, if he listens to the more sober among his advisors they will be heard making plans for what to do should deterrence fail and weapons have to be used. Making just war possible may then appear as feasible as making the fighting of a thermonuclear war feasible (and thereby making deterrence credible).[14] Our statesman may have read in the book just cited an apology for resting the whole defense of the nation at its core upon "the rationality of irrationality." This is defined as follows: "The Rationality of Irrationality war corresponds to a situation in which neither side really believes the issue is big enough to go to war but both sides are willing to use some partial or total committal strategy to force the other side to back down; as a result they may end up in a war that they would not have gone into if either side had realized ahead of time that the other side would not back down even under pressure."[15] A "committal strategy" to make *credible* a nation's resolve to go through with a "rationality of irrationality" policy may be compared to what might work to deter one's opponent in the case of two hot-rod drivers playing the game of "Chicken!" by racing their cars at break-neck speed toward one another, each with his left wheels on the *wrong* side of the white dividing-line in the middle of the road, to see which will give in first and pull over to avoid a collision: one or both drivers might *strap the steering wheel* in order to make it mechanically necessary for him to carry out this irrational action.[16] Thus, Kahn asserts that in this uncertain world "it is just possible that the enemy, in spite of our best thought and preparation, may (either because he is clever, or because he or we have made a miscalculation) develop a technique which *he believes* will destroy more than 80 percent of our strategic forces on the first blow. We wish to assure him that *even if he thinks he can be this successful he is still in serious trouble.* To the extent that he could rely on our using our small remaining force 'sensibly,' this might not be true."[17] Thus, *stabilized* counter-people deterrence, or the supposed technological diversion of this into counter-forces warfare, not only may but, to be maintained, *must be planned* to break down into actual, irrational, purposeless counter-people retaliation. This whole effort to impose limits upon thermonuclear war depends upon the rationality of *committal* to irrational behavior, to which it inevitably returns. Kahn knows very well how alone this can be done: not by contemplating the beauties of the contrivance while it is working to deter surprise attack, but by thinking through and planning our *committal strategy* for when it may not work. "If there were some politically acceptable accident-proof way to make this kind of retaliation completely automatic," he writes, "it would be sensible to put it into immediate effect"; and he unflinchingly calls attention to the fact that the idea of using our forces finally with insensible sensibility against an enemy's society, rather than against his forces, is *not* credible *"unless we really intend to do it.* If we are only *pretending* that we would do it, the credibility and therefore the deterrent value of our force is almost certain to be lessened by the automatic and inevitable leaks. While we can probably keep the details of our war plans secret, it is most unlikely that we can keep the philosophy behind them secret."[18] In other words, to have "the courage of rashness" we must simply strap the wheel; and the stabilization of invulnerable deterrent forces depends on guaranteeing that this has been done, by some determination *equivalent* to the mechanization of the ultimate political-military decision.

Having learned about the rationality of irrational systems, our statesman can be instructed by another sober weapons analyst in what might realistically be called "the virtue of vice" or "the humanity of inhumanity" as the foundation upon which to base this nation's policy, while providing also for the eventuality that such a policy may not be able to be "virtuously" stabilized and therefore may not work. T. C. Schelling believes that it may be virtuous and wise to keep people hostage and integrate the weapons directed at them into plans for preventing a war directed upon them. ". . . Weapons," he writes, "may be more stabilizing and less aggressive if they are capable of civilian reprisal than of military engagement. A standoff between two retaliatory forces is in some ways equivalent to an exchange of hostages; and 'inhumane' weapons, capable of inflicting damage but not able to go after the enemy's strategic forces, *acquire virtue* because of their clearly deterrent function and the lack of temptation they give either side to strike first."[19] This type of arms stabilization depends not so much on formal agreement between the two powers as upon tacit agreement on the part of each to direct its policies to this end. It calls for "mutual arms accommodation" to have and to hold hostages; for "reciprocated unilateral actions and abstentions."[20] Making *decisions,* even some *unilateral* decisions, that this should be the shape of war, of defense and deterrence, lies at the root of the matter. Yet in the end Schelling faces the eventuality that the surface wisdom, virtue, humaneness and rationality of this system may break down and disclose that upon which it is based: purposeless war, vice, inhumanity and irrationality.* He discusses not only the possibility and actuality of an outbreak of thermonuclear war, but also *how on earth* either side can then manage *to surrender,* even *unconditionally* surrender;** and what terms should be exacted of a surrendering enemy. "In the future, at the close of a general war, one might have to allow the conditionally surrendering enemy to retain some retaliatory weapons, these being the only kind that two major powers can use to enforce promises from each other. . . . Certainly more drastic measures than

* Since "commitment" is necessary. In "The Retarded Science of Military Strategy" (*Bulletin of the Atomic Scientists,* March, 1960, 16:103-106), Schelling writes: "We have learned that a threat has to be credible, that credibility may depend (inversely) on the pains of fulfillment for the one who makes the threat, and that to make it credible one has to get 'committed' to its fulfillment." (Or see his *The Strategy of Conflict.* Cambridge, Mass.: Harvard University Press, 1960, p. 6.)

** If under a test suspension or arms control agreement an enemy may not be trusted, why, "in circumstances infinitely more desperate, when a one-hour pause in the war may be of strategic benefit to somebody, if they send us an urgent message acknowledging their guilt in the war and proposing that we preserve our world by letting them surrender to us, are we likely to be able to do anything?" (T. C. Schelling, "Reciprocal Measures for Arms Stabilization," *Daedalus,* Fall, 1960, p. 913.)

any that have yet been considered [to 'safeguard against surprise attack'] might be the minimum requirement of a conditionally surrendering enemy."[21]

Plainly this will not only have to be *allowed,* and allowed a *conditionally* surrendering enemy. This would also be a minimum *requirement,* and a requirement also in the case of an *un*conditionally surrendering enemy, if we are going to stabilize armaments after the war as was attempted before. After deterrence "fails," a future war could then be "prevented" only by basing deterrence again on the preservation of war in its present shape. This gruesome conclusion follows unless we take hopefully reciprocated but yet persistent graduated unilateral steps to make counter-forces warfare possible. No wonder Kenneth Boulding writes: "The grotesque irony of national defense in the nuclear age is that, after having had the inestimable privilege of losing half (or is it three quarters, or all?) our population, we are supposed to set up again the whole system that gave rise to this holocaust!"[22]

The fact is that contemporary weapons analysts are not simply using pure reason, in the form of technical reason wholly stripped of moral *scientia,* in producing their designs for invulnerable weapons systems and arms control. They are using pure reason interfused with moral themes and judgments furnished them by characteristics of the American ethos. They are persuaded by this that it is possible to banish the use of force from human history; and that, when force is used (because of the stupid, aggressive and evil wills of some men) there then supervenes a state of war to which no norms or limits apply. There used to be an oscillation in successive periods of time between all-out peace and all-out (aggressor-defender) war. Contemporary proposals for arms controls based on the total deterrent represent the final product of this ethos. Their distinctiveness is only that they may claim to have banished force and provided in advance for the irrational use of violence in one timeless scheme. There is no hope for purposive political applications of power or for survival unless it is possible to break decisively with this past doctrine of warfare; and, on both counts, in "peace" or in "war," make just war possible.[23] This should become the regulative context of political decision and of the exercise of technical reason in designing weapons, war and deterrence systems, in the present age. There is no other course of action, if, as

President Eisenhower said, the great powers are not "doomed malevolently to eye each other indefinitely across a trembling world." We need fight-the-war plans that are less "deterring," but whose consequences are less catastrophic *when* deterrence fails.

NOTES

1. "The Pacifist Question," *Worldview,* Vol. 3, no. 7-8 (July-August 1960) p. 1.
2. Cf. editorial, *Worldview,* Vol. 2, no. 6 (June 1959), p. 2: ". . . it is more and more agreed that the concept of a 'just war' is an anachronism."
3. *Worldview,* Vol. 3, no. 7-8 (July-August 1960), p. 8.
4. "The Christian Conscience and Weapons of Mass Destruction." The Dun Report of a Special Commission appointed by the Federal Council of the Churches of Christ in America, 1950, pp. 10-11.
5. "Theological and Moral Considerations in International Affairs," background paper for the Fifth World Order Study Conference of the National Council of Churches, in Cleveland, 1958.
6. The Dun Report, *op. cit.,* pp. 10-11.
7. *Ibid.,* p. 12.
8. Calhoun's dissent, *ibid.,* p. 23.
9. *Ibid.,* p. 13 (italics added).
10. *Ibid.,* p. 7.
11. Unpublished paper, American Theological Society, 1960.
12. For more extensive reflections oriented in the direction of national policy decisions, see my *War and the Christian Conscience: How Shall Modern War Be Justly Conducted?* Durham, N.C.: Duke University Press, 1961, pp. 307-324.
13. Herman Kahn, "The Arms Race and Some of its Hazards," *Daedalus,* Fall, 1960, pp. 765-778.
14. Cf. Herman Kahn: *On Thermonuclear War.* Princeton, New Jersey: Princeton University Press, 1960.
15. *Ibid.,* p. 293.
16. *Ibid.,* p. 291. Or see Kahn's article, "The Arms Race and Some of its Hazards," *Daedalus,* Fall, 1960, pp. 756-757.
17. *Ibid.,* p. 185.
18. *Ibid.,* p. 185.
19. "Reciprocal Measures for Arms Stabilization," *Daedalus,* Fall, 1960, p. 892 (italics added).
20. *Ibid.,* p. 904.
21. T. C. Schelling, "Reciprocal Measures for Arms Stabilization," *Daedalus,* Fall, 1960, p. 914.
22. "The Domestic Implications of Arms Control," *Daedalus,* Fall, 1960, p. 858.
23. Cf. Robert M. Tucker: *The Just War: A Study in Contemporary American Doctrine.* Baltimore, Md.: The Johns Hopkins Press, 1960.

Faith
and the perilous future

BY ROGER L. SHINN

ROGER L. SHINN *is Professor of Applied Christianity at Union Theological Seminary, New York. He holds degrees from Heidelberg College, Union Theological Seminary, and Columbia University. From 1949-54 he was Chairman of the Department of Philosophy at Heidelberg College and afterwards for five years on the faculty of the Divinity School of Vanderbilt University. He has lectured widely in American colleges and universities, is one of the editors of* Christianity and Crisis *and the author of several books including* Christianity and the Problem of History; Life, Death, and Destiny; *and* The Existentialist Posture.

Dr. Shinn is a member of the International Relations Committee of the Council for Christian Social Action (United Church of Christ). He is active in the Department of Church and Economic Life and the Department of Racial and Cultural Relations of the National Council of Churches.

Nuclear weapons have by this time blasted many a nostalgic assurance of the past. Time was when we could smile comfortably at Bismarck's saying that there is "a special providence for drunkards, fools, and the United States." The gibe did not sting, because we in the United States were confident. As Max Lerner puts it, "there have been few occasions on which Americans could believe with any conviction in an impending collapse of their social structure and their world."[1] This nation has lived through its history with a strong sense of destiny.

Certainly the Pilgrims acted out of firm belief in their divine vocation. The constitutional fathers, bringing a new nation to birth in an age of enlightenment, sought to lift a beacon of freedom and rationality for mankind. Pioneers conquering a continent gave to society the exultancy of successful adventure. Abraham Lincoln called a country to the high resolve that government of the people should "not perish from the earth." Industrialists built their empires, proclaiming the "gospel of wealth" (Carnegie) or declaring history "bunk" (Ford) because they were sure that they held the keys to progress. Idealists found in the American vision the guarantee of a glorious future in a universe governed by moral law. These various faiths, though differing greatly in intellectual and ethical quality, agreed in expressing a fervent sense of a meaningful future.

Today all these assurances are gone. No one cause explains the deep uncertainties of our time. Yet the destructive power of nuclear warfare has a peculiarly logical force in upsetting man's faith in a purposeful history.

The conflict of conscience over nuclear weapons, as discussed in this book, is a call to responsible action. Nothing in this chapter is intended to mute that call. Mankind faces choices, both technical and moral, and the consequences are momentous.

Nevertheless we may suspect that contemporary decisions take place within a fateful context. Like the chorus of a Greek tragedy we foresee threats without knowing how to remove them, since the very actions designed to help a situation often complicate it still further. Our national and human destinies are not entirely subject to our decisions. It is possible that even the wisest choices of a society may lead to doom. The individual, whose influence on vast matters of policy is slight, has real reasons to feel trapped by events.

Hence the crisis of our time calls for a reconsideration of the traditional questions of fate, of freedom, and of providence—perennial problems now thrust with new urgency upon mankind.

TWILIGHT OF OLD GODS

After the first use of the atomic bomb in 1945 President Truman commented:

> It is an awful responsibility which has come to us.
> We thank God that it has come to us, instead of to our enemies; and we pray that He may guide us to use it in His ways and for His purposes.

Probably most Americans agreed, whatever they might mean by God. Some deity—a power in heaven, the superior intellectual attainments of free men, or the know-how that comes from private enterprise—won the thanks of a grateful people. The achievement of American science and industry reinforced national piety and showed the basic soundness of things.

Much of the world was not so sure. Some Americans shuddered at the "awful responsibility" acknowledged by their President. Winston Churchill described the new scientific knowledge as a "secret long mercifully withheld from man," and many people wished that a merciful providence had withheld it still longer.

Fifteen years after the first nuclear explosions no one in his right mind felt more secure because of modern weapons. Destructive power in human hands had become a threat to belief in a purposeful history and a righteous providence. It threatened equally the secularized notions of providence as technological progress and as national destiny. Today society cannot be very confident about anything connected with the future.

Mankind, it may be said, has often survived threats to its dominant purpose. Many of its greatest achievements have been responses to grave challenges or victories wrought out of intense suffering. Conceivably the present menace may some day appear as another critical stage in a human pilgrimage which has moved through many crises. But there are sound reasons to wonder whether the present emergency is not truly unique.

In past struggles—for all their blundering and waste, their terror and cruelty—suffering was often the occasion for heroic effort. In the worst of destruction, something was saved. If civilizations were destroyed, the human race remained, with other civilizations or tribes untouched by the great debacles. The fall of Assyria or Rome meant no ripple of disturbance in Indonesia, the Congo, or the Americas. Mankind could always look to a future in which the marvelous vitality of germ plasm and the human spirit would achieve new possibilities. Christians, who more than most men felt a sense of the temporary quality of all history, looked forward to an end ordained by God, not an accidental cataclysm caused by human foolishness.

Now the prospects are far more desperate. Presumably a nuclear war in the near future would not wipe out human life, but no continent or island can count itself safe from both blast and radiation. Continued "progress" of technology brings closer the possibility of the destruction of all human life. No longer is the vision of bleak emptiness limited to moods of romantic despair. Soberly factual reasoning readily sees that human history may end in a cataclysm of utter senselessness.

Much of the shock of the human plight comes from the realization that the very activities which formerly increased man's security now undermine it. The centuries of advance in knowledge, which have increased the longevity of individuals, make the life expectancy of the race precarious. Bertrand Russell has observed, "The human race has survived hitherto owing to ignorance and incompetence."[2] With these old guarantees of survival gone, mankind enters a new kind of history. Human survival is less certain than at any time since *homo sapiens* first emerged in the midst of hostile species and a nature he did not understand. Then new knowledge and new powers strengthened his cause. Now, as Werner Heisenberg says, "it is not too crude a simplification of the state of affairs to assert that for the first time in the course of history man on earth faces only himself, that he finds no longer any other partner or foe. . . . In such a confrontation, the extension of technology need no longer be an indication of progress."[3]

Thus history brings us to a stage where traditional forms of confidence in the future are all shaken. Nor can faith count on God to show a way out of the current dilemmas. Trust in God, I shall soon maintain, can be highly meaningful in our time, but no *deus ex machina* promises safety.

One theme in traditional Jewish and Christian faith is that when men are in desperate straits, God does His mighty works of salvation. It is a distortion of that faith to assume that God guarantees survival to any civilization or to mankind. Some have argued in recent years that, if mankind refuses to interfere with the population explosion, God will somehow save us from the resulting disaster. Similarly some may cling to the belief that God has special devices to prevent us from blowing up ourselves and our planet. But neither history nor (I should think) faith support these views. Any honest thinking about human destiny must face the destructive powers now available for the first time.*

CONFLICTING PROVIDENTIAL THEMES

Modern man, skeptical of traditional doctrine, has been credulous enough in seeking substitutes for the orthodox belief in providence. He has tried Hegel's theory that history, though ruthless to individuals, is the triumphant march of the *Weltgeist* toward the goal of freedom. He has taken comfort from Adam Smith's notion of an "invisible hand" that regulates society so that the aims of various groups somehow work for the general good. He has seized Marx's idea of a historical dialectic that drives history through cataclysms to a better

* The Christian belief in providence is currently the subject of international discussions. The Division of Studies of the World Council of Churches, in a proposal for a major study, says that "the age-old problem of Providence and history" has "special urgency today in view of the many catastrophic events which have occurred, the rapidity of the changes which have taken place and man's consequent intellectual confusion and spiritual need." *Bulletin,* Division of Studies, World Council of Churches, Vol. VI, No. 2 (Autumn, 1960), pp. 25-26.

The events which prompt the study include, of course, many besides the spread of nuclear weapons. But the new powers of destruction (along with the population explosion) are probably the most unprecedented of the historical changes of our epoch.

society. He has lived by faith in inevitable progress—either Comte's reliance on the arrival of the "positive age" of science or Spencer's assurance that nature drives man toward perfection. He has counted on a moral law that guarantees the ultimate triumph of righteous causes—usually the causes of the believer. These various creeds belong not only to intellectual theorists; they have stirred modern political and economic history.

The fateful character of nuclear destruction is to threaten equally *all* these faiths. Neither capitalistic nor Communistic dogma predicted disaster on the modern world-wide scale. Neither metaphysical theories nor wistful reliance on science prepared men for the contemporary ordeal.

Somewhere behind all these beliefs lies the biblical faith in a meaningful history under God. The modern substitutes for providence may contradict the biblical belief or modify it beyond recognition, but they share its basic insistence that man lives in a history that has value and direction. Hence the contemporary alarm, when it has not led to radical atheism, has sometimes turned people to Zen Buddhism and other Oriental faiths which do not affirm the importance of history.

Yet the deeply historical character of Jewish and Christian faith remains influential in Western culture. The current crisis thrusts before traditional faith the questions of our time. Such encounter never simply confirms orthodox doctrine, but it often discovers new vitality in traditional faith.

Any fresh look at the biblical faith in providence sees the interplay, sometimes the conflict, between two motifs. The first of these finds evidence everywhere in history of the sovereignty of a righteous, purposeful God. The second knows only the hidden workings of God, concealed from the observer but occasionally revealed in unexpected ways to faith.

The first motif recurs frequently in a variety of forms. Sometimes it is the belief that God will protect His chosen people—or at least the city of Jerusalem—from the historical disasters that strike down other people. At other times the belief acquires a moral quality, as biblical writers try to correlate the righteousness of kings with the prosperity of society. When facts refute the beliefs, people turn to the messianic hope for a new king who will restore the ancient glories of David.

Although these ideas in their traditional language sound quaint today, their secular counterparts are common in American literature.

The doctrine of the chosen people has been revised by many writers, among them Henry Luce, who has proposed that America uniquely among nations is immune to the decay which has stricken all the great empires of the past. The belief in moral law that favors freedom and justice has echoed from many national leaders, among whom John Foster Dulles was more notable and sincere than most. And the mystical hope in a messianic leader who will resolve our perplexities resounds in political oratory every fourth year.

The same Bible that voices these various providential beliefs also brings radical criticism against them all. The great prophets challenge the confidence of the chosen people, insisting that God has chosen them for a service which promises no safety. Without denying the righteousness of God, some of the prophets point to events that refute any clear doctrine of moral retribution. The Isaiah of the exile (Isaiah 40-55) proclaims a God who hides himself—a God who is Lord of history but whose ways are not our ways and whose acts are un-recognizable by the nations. The Psalmists and wisdom writers pour out their doubts about any meaningful patterns of history. Job acknowl-edges a God of utter mystery. The apocalypses see history in such straits that no messianic son of David, but only a being from heaven, can put things in order.

In this setting Jesus appears and is hailed as Lord and Messiah (Christ). His disciples and apostles announce the revelation of the sovereign God in a man crucified. At his death his enemies jeer, "He saved others; he cannot save himself. He is the King of Israel; let him come down now from the cross, and we will believe in him" (Matt. 27:42). If this is providential power, certainly it is hidden power. All attempts of piety to make sense of the workings of God in history must come to terms with the crucifixion of Jesus.

But questioning and thinking go on. The human mind must look for some way to read "the signs of the times." So Christians have tried repeatedly to relate their faith in God's activity in Christ to the pano-rama of history. Jews, Christians, and secularists have searched past and present for clues that history is meaningful or that men can so plan their actions as to make it meaningful.

Throughout the centuries since the crucifixion of Christ, the two motifs of the Bible have continued their interplay in the consciousness of Western man. Sometimes the issues have become articulate in care-ful debate. More often men have faced them in vaguer thoughts and feelings, as events have prompted hope or despair. The nineteenth century brought the conflict into sharper focus than any preceding age. This was the century in which Comte, Hegel, Marx, and Spencer spun out their grandiose theories of a "providential" history heading in the right direction. It was also the century of Schopenhauer, Nietzsche, and other apostles of romantic despair, who denounced all the optimistic dogmas.

The nineteenth century often debated the issue in specifically religious or moral terms. Victor Hugo in 1862 described the Battle of Waterloo and affirmed his belief:

> Was it possible that Napoleon should win this battle? We answer no. Why? Because of Wellington? Because of Blücher? No. Because of God.
>
> It was time that this vast man should fall.
>
> The excessive weight of this man in human destiny disturbed the equilibrium. . . . The moment had come for incorruptible supreme equity to look to it. . . .
>
> Napoleon had been impeached before the Infinite, and his fall was decreed.
>
> He vexed God.
>
> Waterloo is not a battle; it is the change of front of the universe.[4]

Behind that ringing prose is the weighty tradition both of Greek tragedy and of *one* providential motif in biblical thought. But before Victor Hugo wrote the words, Søren Kierkegaard had bitterly attacked any idea of providence that claimed to understand the mystery of God and His ways with men. About the same time Fyodor Dostoevsky (despite his Russian messianism) was posing the choice between nihilism and apocalypse. Either alternative denied any meaningful pattern of history. Nihilism rejected God; apocalypse affirmed a faith despite the confusions of history.

Thus the twentieth century brought a divided heritage to the new problem posed for mankind by the terror of nuclear warfare.

FATE AND ACCIDENT

Every person—skeptic or believer—must seek to make some kind of sense out of history if he would live sanely in it. Today even the most secular analysis of contemporary society—e.g., of colonialism or of the racial problem in the United States—is likely to find *some* evidence of present retribution for past wrongs or of tides of history that are shaping the future. If history were *complete* chaos, no historian could write the results of research. He would have no criteria for distinguishing and reporting the important rather than the trivial. If *nothing* about history were predictable, there could be no political or international wisdom. The hallucinations of a psychotic would have as much validity as the best statesmanship. Any person's reading of the daily newspaper depends upon an assumption that events in history fit somehow into rational comprehension. Yet historians are increasingly reluctant to find any clear pattern, certainly any moral pattern of cosmic scope.

The man of faith, inheriting the two biblical motifs, finds the hiddenness of God overwhelmingly persuasive for our time. It may be that another age will make sense out of what looks like confusion to us. Conceivably a future Milton will write an epic of man's twentieth century struggles in order to "justify the ways of God to man." But in our present perplexities we cannot project our insights that far.

The burden of contemporary man is to live under the double threat of a hostile fate and of sheer accident. *Fate* appears in the compulsion upon more and more nations to acquire nuclear weapons. Even if some miracle of statesmanship should lead to a genuine agreement between the United States and the Soviet Union, other nations are determined to join the nuclear club. This compulsive process increases the likelihood of *accident*. If humanity turns the globe into cinders or poisons the atmosphere disastrously, it will not do so by direct intention. Some bluff, some miscalculation will set off the holocaust. As more and more nations acquire the new weapons, the chance of accidental nuclear warfare increases from possibility to probability to virtual certainty.[5]

The element of fate was evident in the first use of the atomic bomb on Hiroshima. Albert Einstein, when he first advised President Roosevelt to start working on atomic weapons, did so with a tortured conscience. Einstein's pacifist inclinations wrestled with his fear that the Nazis might achieve such a weapon and dominate the world. The United States built the bomb as a defense, lest someone else build it first. But when the bomb was ready to use, Nazi Germany was conquered. The remaining enemy was Japan, already wobbling toward defeat, but still able to kill our soldiers. Given the fateful necessities of human history, it was almost inevitable that we should use the new weapon in a way never intended by those who first urged its production.

The same fate combined with accident in the second use of the bomb on Nagasaki. Kokura, the target for the day, was covered by clouds. The plane circled that city for nearly fifty minutes and actually attempted three bombing runs, but the city remained hidden. A malfunctioning gasoline pump required hasty action. The plane flew on to Nagasaki and there released the bomb.[6] Out of such accidents of weather and machinery came the destruction of one city's 80,000 persons rather than another's.

Future accidents will be far vaster in scope. The future of nations or of humanity may depend on this strange combination of fate and accident: the fate that drives the arms race to ever more disastrous proportions despite the rational forebodings of the leaders of the Soviet Union and the United States, and the blundering accident that may send the weapons into motion.

PROVIDENCE AND THE UNKNOWN FUTURE

In such a situation any belief in providence, whether in religious terms or in the secular substitutes we have noted, is clearly an act of faith, not an inductive conclusion from the evidence. But even the most daring faith must somehow relate itself to man's knowledge of life. Although profound faith always acknowledges mystery in existence, yet the believer must have some notion of what he means by his belief.

Some able writers deny that modern man has any business thinking providentially. Karl Löwith sees all the modern secular substitutes for providence as foolish illusions, and he all but denies that Christianity rightly has a doctrine of providence. Of the New Testament he says, "The importance of secular history decreases in direct proportion to the intensity of man's concern with God and himself. . . . The message of the New Testament is not an appeal to historical action but to repentance."[7] Although such sentences might seem to come from a pietist or a mystic, Löwith himself is an acute student of modern society.

Paul Tillich, without ever going quite so far as Löwith, sometimes comes very close to this theme. "Providence is not a theory about some activities of God; it is the religious symbol of the courage of confidence with respect to fate and death."[8] Such a definition is eminently appropriate for a nuclear age. Yet it surrenders a great deal. Biblical faith certainly does declare "some activities of God." To describe faith without reference to the course of world history is to abandon a conviction prominent in historical Christianity and in its many secular echoes in the Western world.

Perhaps the events of our day, portentous though they are, do not utterly destroy the providential outlook upon world history. There are honest hopes—chastened but real hopes—related to actual historical possibilities. These are not certainties, not *the* Christian hope, in the sense of the assurance on which faith stands or falls. But they need not be. Man, though never certain about future events, yet has the responsibility to live, to work, and to plan.

Providential faith has always pointed to new possibilities in history. Although the weight of the past is heavy, deadlocks do sometimes break, impasses end, unforeseen opportunities emerge. The voices of doom have not always been accurate. The legacies of hatred from World War II—e.g., between France and Germany or between the United States and Japan—have been transcended to a far greater degree than we might have thought possible in so short a time. The reconciliation is not a proof of health, since it depends so largely on shared fear of the Communist nations. But the example shows that history is not so rigid nor the future so closed as to deny unexpected possibilities.

Today, as in times past, there are possibilities, dim but real, of wise statecraft or of generous acts which can break the chains of guilt and terror. Erich Fromm sees some such possibilities for human behavior. Christian orthodoxy is less confident of human nature, but never gives up on the possibilities of God's grace in men's lives.

Conceivably the new means of destruction may drive the twentieth century out of its tribalism into some better realization of the unity of man. The classical faith in providence has always held that, even in the most deserved suffering among the worst of men, divine judgment is never simply vindictive. Its purpose is always redemptive. Possibly the very terror of our age and the sufferings past and future may be the means of revelation to men of their common nature and their need of each other. A courageous faith will neither exaggerate this hope nor renounce it.

Even the most sober judgment of the future has no right to assert that total war is inevitable. Predictions of such a war usually assume two steps: (1) someone will trigger the war, probably by miscalculation or accident; (2) the forces of instant retaliation will swiftly involve the whole globe. The increase of nuclear weapons makes Step 1 increasingly likely (as discussed above). But Step 1 does not *necessarily* produce Step 2. There is even the possibility that, as Step 1 becomes more likely, the restraints upon Step 2 are increasing.*

Certainly one of the most hopeful signs to come from the Pentagon recently has been the repeated indication of a new strategy of "controlled response" to enemy attack rather than "massive retaliation." Some advocates of disarmament will reject this judgment. They consider all nuclear warfare so horrible that they can make no distinctions between better and worse possibilities. But our world cannot afford the luxury of discarding such distinctions. Such a change in war plans may be more important for mankind than the grander but less likely dreams of total disarmament.

The leaders of the two great nuclear powers are well aware of the nature of modern warfare. They are ready to keep playing a risky game, but they have no intention of unloosing the big war. As more and more nations, with less to lose, acquire the new weapons, the chance of rash acts increases. But the very distribution of power changes the world from a rivalry of two vast armed camps, each afraid of and ready to annihilate the other. A more pluralistic world, with its interplay of many national groups, each seeking a variety of friends and allies from time to time, may be safer than a world of two great powers driven by irreconcilable ideologies. Clearly a world in which rivalries are not magnified into vast systems of hate allows a more open future than a world in which one rigid hostility dominates international policies.

An asset in the foreboding future is the inherent tenacity of man and the fecundity of life. When art and philosophy express a mordant spirit, the bloodstream courses on and the glands continue their work.

---

* Thus Hanson Baldwin has analyzed in some detail the ways in which dispersion of nuclear weapons, while increasing in some respects the world's instability, may in other respects make for greater stability than we have in the present bi-polar world. "If Sixteen Countries Had the Bomb," *The New York Times Magazine*, Feb. 12, 1961.

These, no less than the mind, are part of man's created nature. If war comes, probably some, perhaps many, will survive. (The sooner it comes, we may ironically note, the less possible is total disaster.) The lot of the living will not be enviable. Most of us, when we think rationally about the subject, would rather die in the first blow than outlast the nuclear slaughter. But if the event comes, some will act otherwise. Their future will be laborious, painful, bitter. But conceivably from what we call "underdeveloped" areas of the world may come new impulses to undertake again, under dreadful handicaps, the pilgrimage of civilization.

All this talk of the future, of course, is speculation. We can neither deny nor take heart from such conjectures. Our future is as uncharted as was the Western hemisphere when Columbus sailed. Some of his critics expected Columbus to sail off the edge of the world. Their predictions may get tardy fulfilment in a human race plunging off the end of history into death. The worst may come: mankind may destroy itself, or so much of itself and its earth that no one can take courage from the future.*

EARTH IS NOT ALL

The worst possibilities remind us that providential faith, without writing off history as unimportant, has never limited its interest to the history of this world. If the pressure of events rightly forces the most transcendental faith to look at the hard facts of history, faith in turn prompts earthbound calculation to lift its eyes beyond immediate horizons.

---

* Hans Morgenthau has expressed with bitter eloquence the meaning of nuclear destruction to a world that has lost faith in any transcendent meaning of its history:

"Sacrificial death has meaning only as the outgrowth of an individual decision which chooses death over life. . . . There is, then, a radical difference in meaning between a man risking death by an act of will and fifty million people simultaneously reduced—by somebody switching a key thousands of miles away—to radioactive ashes, indistinguishable from the ashes of their houses, books, and animals. . . .

"We think and act as though the possibility of nuclear death had no bearing upon the meaning of life and death. . . . Yet the possibility of nuclear death, by destroying the very meaning of life and death, has reduced to absurd clichés the noble words of yesterday. To defend freedom and civilization is absurd if nobody is left to honor the dead. The very conceptions of honor and shame require a

Mankind, now aware that destruction may be imminent, also realizes better than in the past that this earth is not all of God's universe. Perhaps it is "providential" that the first generation to doubt its global future with such scientific logic is also the first generation to think with fascination about the probability of life on other planets.

Even so, there is small comfort in the notion that the wreck of *this* history is not the wreck of all life and history. This history is all we know. The possibility of a superior form of life and history a hundred light years distant does nothing to redeem our history. That is why men have always been more concerned with God's eternity than with God's geography.

The fashions of our time do not allow much speculation about eternity. With a mixture of skepticism and modesty, we refrain from descriptions of a future heaven and hell. We see that we can have no charts to eternity, and that the charts of our ancestors were often a crude combination of wishful and fearful thinking.

Yet Christian faith believes in God's eternity. His purposes are certainly not limited to this time and planet. In one of the great statements of providential faith St. Paul writes: "For the wages of sin is death, but the free gift of God is eternal life in Christ Jesus our Lord" (Romans 6:23). Present history confirms the first half of that sentence, even in its most literal meaning. The second half clearly is not intended to be a promise of historical survival. The Christian faith in providence includes eternal life. Those who trust in God feel no compulsion to fill in the details.

The dominant secular philosophies have their own echoes of this Christian trust. Even in this positivistic age few would maintain that the sole purpose of life is survival. If that were the case, every life would fail in its purpose. So would the life of mankind, for it takes no nuclear age to tell us that this planet cannot maintain life forever.

Thus every attempt to find meaning in the concrete events of life drives men to seek something more than the visible. Yet no solace in

---

society that knows what honor and shame mean." (See "Death in the Nuclear Age," *Commentary,* September, 1961, pp. 231-34.)

Morgenthau rightly observes that mankind has not yet taken in the meaning of this new situation. He regards this failure as "the saving grace of our age," because the truth would bring us to despair. But perhaps the same truth may drive us to reconsider the meaning of classical faith, even when many of the literal formulations of that faith are no longer possible.

eternity can take the sting out of defeat of the human enterprise. Any
large scale nuclear war will be a powerful blow to the best purposes
and aspirations of historical man. That is the peril within which our
generation must live. Hendrik Kraemer refers to "human history as
God's risky adventure with man."⁹ The risk is real. History is no
shadow play in which actors in safety seem to live dangerously.

Facing the hazards of our time, we have the right and duty to ask
whether trust in divine providence any longer makes sense. Perhaps
only those who ask the question in all its poignancy can understand an
answer. But those who do ask may approach an answer in the awareness that the most influential human faith in providence has centered
in the cross of Christ. If God was active there, bringing healing out of
that evil and pain, men had better not set limits on His power. If "in
Christ God was reconciling the world to Himself," He can continue to
do so even in nuclear destruction.

If worst comes to worst, as may actually happen, faith—though the
faith of dying men—will say these things:

God is not the doer of these deeds. Evil is always defiance of His will.

Yet God is in the midst even of destruction. He is the creator of
nature with its awesome energies, creator of the order by which
causes lead to effects, creator of the men whose skills build
weapons.

And God, as at Golgotha, suffers in the world's agonies and loves
the world which can defy but not conquer Him.

PERILOUS LIVING

Out of his long diplomatic experience and his Christian faith,
George F. Kennan has written: "Here our main concern must be to
see that man, whose own folly once drove him from the Garden of
Eden, does not now commit the blasphemous act of destroying,
whether in fear or in anger or in greed, the great and lovely world in
which, even in his fallen state, he has been permitted by the grace of
God to live."¹⁰

No past generation has ever faced that problem. To men who live in
the "risky adventure" of our age, providential faith brings an awareness of this new vocation. To trust providence offers no safety from
pain, no escape from the world's troubles. It may involve men the

more completely in the struggles and insecurities of history. Yet it has a helpful practical meaning which can be stated in two affirmations.

(1) Fate and accident are not absolute masters. Men have the opportunity by their decisions to influence the future.

(2) Not everything depends upon human wisdom and activity. Men are not wise to seek infallible leaders for every crisis or scapegoats for every failure.

Men of faith will hope that by the grace of God both some who believe in God and some who do not may share in the fruits of providential faith. In an unpredictable future almost the only certainty is that every society faces perils and frustrations. American society, powerful and traditionally confident, faces special difficulties in learning to live in a new kind of world. The temptations to both fatalism and fanaticism are great.

Both are evident in national politics. Fatalism reasons that foreign aid has not stopped Communist gains, that efforts at negotiation have been futile. So it underestimates the possibilities of responsible decisions. It refuses to accept the burden of continued effort and taxation, and it renounces the opportunities that history offers a nation, even in fateful times. Fanaticism believes that fervent activities can manipulate history and exorcise "the enemy." Hence it neglects solid activity for the sake of frantic gestures, as in the movements of McCarthyism and of the John Birch Society. In the process it feeds the very prejudices and irrationalities that invite destruction.

Against such misguided alternatives providential faith is a call to purposeful activity. In telling us that we are neither lords of history nor puppets, it tells us the same of our fellow creatures on earth. From its perspective we see our adversaries as creatures too. While opposing their aggressive designs, we can understand their anxieties, which often resemble our own. We would rather live in this world with rivals than destroy them, even if the latter policy were not dangerous to ourselves. We can understand the desire of neutrals to base policy on their national interest rather than ours. In some such ways faith, which does not itself dictate political judgments, may contribute to a humane wisdom which makes policy.

Once before in human history a great civilization lost its sense of meaningful destiny. Philosophers declared that "Whirl is king," and popular cults worshiped the goddess of chance, called *Tyche* or *For-*

tuna. Then a faith in providence, stemming from the cross of Christ, opened a new era of history—not an age of purity, for history never offers that, but a time when men could again live in some confidence.

We cannot expect history to repeat itself. The future offers no prospect of re-establishing traditional Christendom, and few of us would want that. But precedent offers some hope, though the evidence at this moment is slim, that God may grant a tired world a fresh spirit to meet an age of history which no man can foresee.

NOTES

1. Max Lerner, *America as a Civilization*. New York: Simon and Schuster, 1957, p. 705.
2. Bertrand Russell, *The Impact of Science on Society*. New York: Simon and Schuster, 1953, p. 97.
3. Werner Heisenberg, in *Symbolism in Religion and Literature,* ed. by Rollo May. New York: Braziller, 1960, p. 226.
4. Victor Hugo, *Les Misérables,* tr. by Charles E. Wilbour. New York: Modern Library, n.d., "Cosette," Book I, Ch. 9, pp. 279-80.
5. See Harrison Brown and James Real, *Community of Fear* (Santa Barbara, California: Center for the Study of Democratic Institutions, 1960). C. P. Snow, Hanson Baldwin, and others have made the same point persuasively.
6. The account, as given to United Press International by a crew member, was printed in *The New York Times,* August 14, 1960.
7. Karl Löwith, *Meaning in History*. Chicago: University of Chicago Press, 1949, pp. 192, 196.
8. Paul Tillich, *The Courage To Be*. New Haven: Yale University Press, 1952, p. 168.
9. *The Communication of the Christian Faith*. Philadelphia: Westminster Press, 1956, p. 13.
10. George F. Kennan, "Foreign Policy and Christian Conscience," *Atlantic Monthly,* Vol. 203, No. 5 (May, 1959), p. 49.

A reading list

Bainton, Roland H.: *Christian Attitudes Toward War and Peace*. Abingdon Press, 1960. (An authoritative history of the subject.)

Batchelder, Robert C.: *The Irreversible Decision, 1939-1950*. Houghton Mifflin, 1961.

Brown, Harrison and Real, James: *The Community of Fear*. Published by the Fund for the Republic, 1960.

Butterfield, Herbert: *International Conflict in the Twentieth Century—A Christian View*. Harper & Brothers, 1960.

Clancy, William (Editor): *The Moral Dilemma of Nuclear Weapons*. Pamphlet published by the Church Peace Union, 1961.

Fromm, Erich: *May Man Prevail?* A Doubleday Anchor Book, 1961.

Herz, John H.: *International Politics in the Atomic Age*. Columbia University Press, 1959.

Jaspers, Karl: *The Future of Mankind*. The University of Chicago Press, 1961.

Jungk, Robert: *Brighter Than a Thousand Suns*. Harcourt, Brace, 1958.

Kahn, Herman: *On Thermonuclear War*. Princeton University Press, 1960.

Kennan, George F.: *Russia and the West Under Lenin and Stalin*. Little, Brown, 1961.

Kissinger, Henry A.: *The Necessity for Choice*. Harper & Brothers, 1960.

Nagle, William J. (Editor): *Morality and Modern Warfare*. Helicon Press, 1960. (This volume contains an extensive bibliography of books and articles.)

Ramsey, Paul: *War and the Christian Conscience*. Duke University Press, 1961.

Thompson, Charles S. (Editor): *Morals and Missiles*. James Clarke, London, 1959.

Thompson, Kenneth W.: *Christian Ethics and the Dilemmas of Foreign Policy*. Duke University Press, 1959.

Toynbee, Philip (Editor): *The Fearful Choice*. Wayne State University Press, 1959.

Tucker, Robert W.: *The Just War—A Study in Contemporary American Doctrine*. The Johns Hopkins Press, 1960.

Index of major issues
discussed by more than one author